Evolve

Transmute • Transform • Transcend

One's guide to spiritual evolution in the Universe

FIRST PRINCIPLE – FIRST NATIONS ACKNOWLEDGEMENT

One acknowledges the many and diverse First Nations in Australia (Aboriginal and Torres Strait Islander) and on Earth as the traditional custodians of Country (land, sea* and sky) and the ongoing living connections (mind–body–spirit) to the land, waters (salt/fresh), kin and community. One pays One's respect to One's spiritual ancestors and Elders past, present and emerging. One honours the spirit in One and all sentient Beings on the planet and in the universe.

* Throughout this book, all references to 'sea' include all bodies of water.

Everything is Connected – All is One

First published in Australia in 2023 by:
Author: Shawn Wondunna-Foley
Innerway PO Box 2141
Hervey Bay QLD 4655 Australia
innerway.com.au

Copyright © Shawn Wondunna-Foley 2023

All rights reserved. This book is copyright. Apart from any fair dealings for the purposes of private study, research, criticism or review permitted under the Australian Copyright Act 1968, no part may be stored or reproduced by any process without prior written permission. Enquiries should be made to the publisher.

ISBN: 978-0-6455073-2-4

 A catalogue record for this book is available from the National Library of Australia

Cover image: iStock/johan63
Front cover design: Lorna Hendry and Shawn Wondunna-Foley
Editing and layout: Lorna Hendry
Typeset in Amiri, A-Space, Gotham and Gtek Technology
Printing: Ingram Sparks

EVOLVE

Transmute • Transform • Transcend

One's guide to spiritual evolution in the Universe

Shawn Wondunna-Foley

Disclaimer

The information in this book is meant to give general advice on spiritual enlightenment and mindful living interests only. Although the author tried to make sure the quotes and information in the book are correct and from reliable sources, the author and publisher are not responsible for any mistakes or problems that may occur from using the information. This information is provided 'as is', without any guarantees of accuracy, completeness, or timeliness. No warranties, expressed or implied, are given regarding the information's performance, quality, or suitability for a particular purpose. If you make a decision or take action based on the information in this book, the author, publisher or their partners, corporations, agents or employees won't be held responsible for any negative consequences, special damages or similar problems that may occur, even if they were warned about the possibility of such problems.

Preface

One set out to inspire other truth finders and co-create a better world on Earth through One's website (innerway.com.au), quotes and books. This small action began in 2017 and is part of a larger unfolding manifestation and evolving process involving everyone on the planet. The intentional outcome of this personal call to action is that it will eventually cause a global tsunami of inner change in human consciousness. The tipping point for planetary change to a new interstellar spiritually united Type 1 civilisation requires only 1 per cent of all people living on Earth to align in coherence with a new vibrational reality to enable significant change for all of humanity. One has always known that 'as an indomitable spirit One has a cosmic responsibility' to bring 'truth and the light of spirit, soul or cosmic consciousness' to this planet so that it will benefit all future generations.

One has always known the truth about oneself but was most likely too afraid to believe it. Now is the time to embrace One's inner self-awareness and reveal the truth of who One is to oneself. This truth is undeniable and an inevitable part of the process of spiritual evolution of all humans on Earth.

The truth which One is unable to escape in this life or the next is that One is and has always been a spirit, soul or cosmic consciousness.

One knew when One began this journey that it was One's responsibility to share One's great thoughts, teachings, learnings, pointings, ideas, beliefs, words and books with the world. As part of this process, One had to first create a different space within One's mind that was designed to encourage a new language and new perspective of the world that One lives in today.

So, One created a way to reach out to everyone and give individuals the tools to empower and create the best version of oneself. A way to put One's best works into the hands of millions of people, with very little in One's way. This book is an abbreviated encapsulation of One's guiding principles, thoughts and beliefs. As One's messages continue to grow and are shared around the world, One hopes that these ideas or memes will rise above the white noise of egoic life and serve each new person in co-creating a better version of oneself. One's purpose is to collectively manifest a new reality on Earth today.

If One is new here, welcome. Although the outcomes of this book are important, it is really One's inner belief in oneself and One's positive energy that will make a difference in One's own life and future generations. Thanks for being here. Let us all make good choices to co-create great changes that will benefit billions on Earth now.

> **Change begins the moment One looks inside oneself and realises who One truly is in this world and One's place in the universe.**

How to use this book

This book is about realising the light, love and oneness within oneself so One can benefit all people on Earth. It is about aligning with a new vibration to manifest a new life on the planet for the next 100 to 1000 years. It is accepting that things are the way they appear to be because of humanity's current egoic construct, false identities, global patterns of separation, fear, greed, lack of a shared vision, absence of personal responsibility, hateful attitudes, mistrust and deception, focused selfishness, the pursuit of power, interpersonal violence, unhealthy relationships, toxic lifestyles, destructive desires, consumer materialism, addictive attachments, economic slavery, resistance to change and egoic mental matrix of successive generations.

The spiritual source code for life, the universe and everything cannot be found by seeking it. It can only be actualised by knowing it within oneself here and now on the planet. It lives within each and every sentient Being's spirit, soul or cosmic consciousness on Earth. Do not search outside of oneself to discover the secrets of living a joyful, peaceful and contented life. Simply look within to realise the divine light of existence within One's infinite Being.

One's mission should One choose to accept it is not to 'fix the world'. This is a shared and intergenerational responsibility. Instead, focus on co-creating the best version of oneself and allow this act of positive alignment to ripple out into the world and universe wherever One is now. One's positive energy is like a raindrop of inspiration that will eventually join with others on the planet and become an ocean of collective consciousness and critical change. Never underestimate One's individual power and ability to change oneself from within and the world around One now.

Life is only now. It can never be yesterday or tomorrow. These are only concepts. One of the worst things is to miss the recognition of your own good fortune. You are life itself and the One witnessing it.
Mooji

The universe works in wonderful and mysterious ways. This might seem counterintuitive at first but trust the process and believe in a reality where One's existence is integral to an interstellar spiritually based Type 1 civilisation. Where One's life is not based on maintaining an egoic life support system but part of an interconnected and aligned conscious awareness for prosperity, abundance, awakened living and being on Earth.

As One reads this book, One will gain a greater understanding of the choices One will make about working, living, playing and being on Country (land, sea and sky) as part of One's planetary citizenship. It is also about learning to be mindful of the way One thinks, speaks and acts with regard to these important decisions on a daily basis. Not as a human being, but as a spiritual sentient Being of the universe on Earth. Mainly, it's about how not to become overwhelmed or distracted now that One is here. One's first-priority mission is to become awake. Everything else that follows from this moment will be revealed to One like the open sky on a cloudless day. Simply stay present in a state of expanded awareness.

For more information, there's an official website (www.innerway.com.au). Look for information that will support One's spiritual life journey and assist One to co-create a better version of oneself. This book is on the web, so you can purchase or download it. Once One has enjoyed reading it, help make life better for other people. Share One's ideas about new sections, or changes to the existing ones. Add to the useful terms or make comments about how the content can be improved and reach a greater audience. One is open to receiving positive feedback and constructive suggestions. From this information One will collectively review the ideas and changes and fold them into future revisions.

Dedication

This book is dedicated to everyone who believes in the idea of vibrational alignment and attracting prosperity, abundance and an awakened living future on the planet. A future that is lived in the present through committing One's mind–body–spirit to a vision greater than oneself. It is a shared vision of an interstellar spiritually based Type 1 civilisation that completely changes One's existing relationships with oneself, each other, the world and interstellar Beings in the universe. It is time now to answer a spiritual call to action. The universe invites One to manifest a new level of cosmic consciousness, new life, new experiences, new reality and new Earth.

When One chooses to embrace the unknown without fear, One moves forward with a belief and trust in the universe that rises above humanity's egoic construct, sociocultural programming and obsolete coding. It is learning how to go into the storm of chaos in One's life and the world to find the central point of stillness, silence and serenity. Within this space, One is capable of nurturing and nourishing the inner courage to speak the truth, act with integrity and be authentic. Simplicity is the solution to the complexities of life as One knows it.

A change of spiritual consciousness is coming; in fact, it is already here. This book is part of the process that supports the spiritual evolution on the planet and conscious engagement with other interstellar sentient Beings in the galaxy.

One is integral to the collective consciousness of humanity as it evolves into a higher vibration of mindful working, prosperous living and awakened being. This is all within the experience of One's individual realised awakening.

The closer One moves to align with One's spirit, soul or cosmic consciousness, the faster the collective consciousness on the planet will reach a tipping point of dynamic and accelerated change in the world. What will flow from this moment onwards will truly astound and amaze One. It will be beyond One's wildest imagination and transcend One's current beliefs, thinking and reality on the planet.

Know that the consciousness of One's Being is not a problem to be solved but a reality to be experienced.

The future is unfolding toward the conscious evolution of all of humankind. As One accepts this destiny, One will become aligned with this newly manifested reality now.

Peace, Love and Freedom

Shawn
Hervey Bay, Queensland, Australia

First Nations have always had an intimate knowing and intangible connection to spirit. It is something that lives within everyone and Country (land, sea and sky). To live without spirit is like trying to breathe without air.

About the author

Shawn Wondunna-Foley, a Butchulla (*Badtjala*) First Nation Australian author and public speaker, is a multi-talented individual. He serves as a positive thought leader, street artist, creative designer, spiritual lifestyle coach, cultural advisor and philanthropist. Currently working as a public servant, Shawn has a deep love for Country (land, sea, and sky) and values the arts, culture and community of Hervey Bay on the Fraser Coast in Queensland, Australia where he lives, works and plays.

Shawn has written two cultural heritage books – *The Badtjala People* and *I on Country* – and several books on mindfulness, wellness and spiritual consciousness, including *One, Two, Three, Awaken* and *Infinite Existence*. All these books serve as inspiring resources and gifts for those seeking inner guidance and a more enlightened way of life in the world.

His latest work, *Evolve: Transmute – Transform – Transcend*, is a guide to spiritual evolution in the universe. This book offers readers a path to inner change, self-realisation, and divine awakening. It encourages all to break free and embrace the light, love, and oneness within One's sentient Being.

Shawn believes: *Everything is connected – All is one.* Everyone is spiritually entangled in an ocean of conscious existence with all other sentient Beings in the universe. *Evolve* is a tribute to this belief and serves as a guide to help individuals transmute, transform, and transcend One's personal pain and suffering to evolve into a 'Bright' or awake Being on Earth.

Read Shawn's blog and connect with him on his website innerway.com.au. One is also invited to click on the resources at innerway.com.au/freeresources, which support this book and Shawn's learning, teachings and pointings.

Be One Now

One simple moment of spiritual realisation.
One divine awakening for all of humankind.

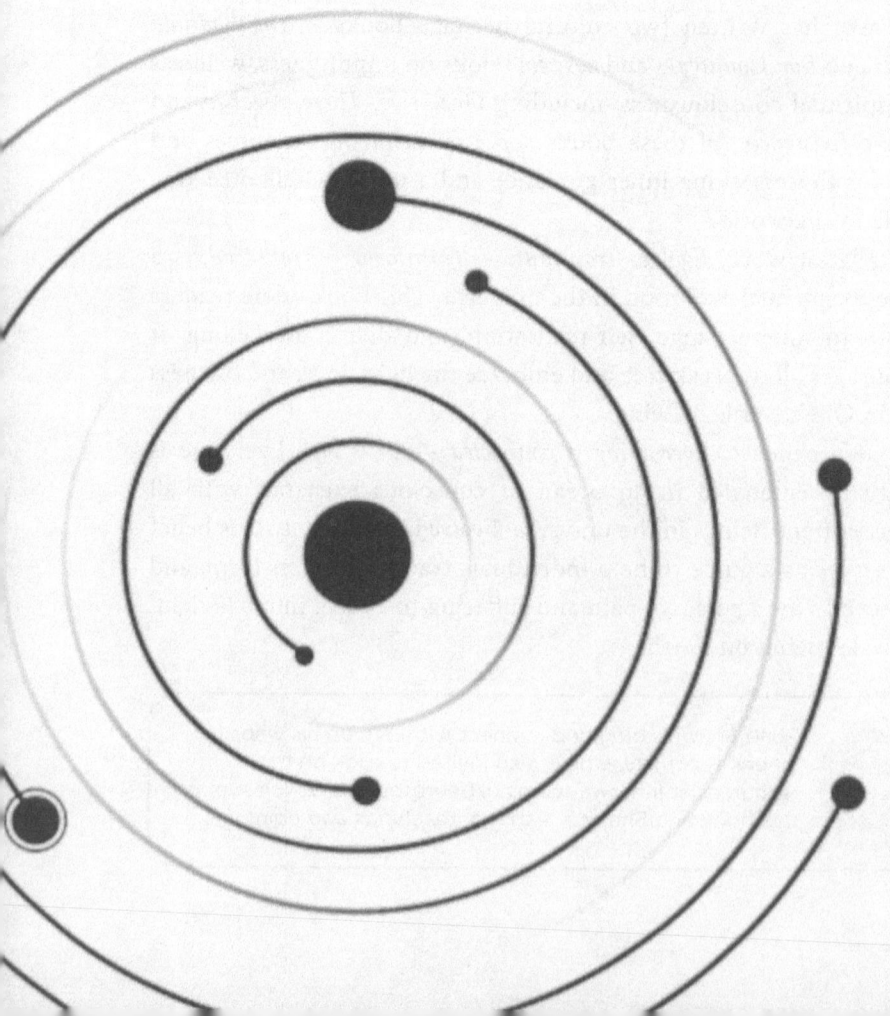

Contents

Important note: Language of Spirit or 'One' 2
Useful terms 4
Introduction 13

Part 1: Welcome to Earth 23
Part 2: Spirit, soul or cosmic consciousness 57
Part 3: Transmute One's spiritual existence 87
Part 4: Transform One's mind-body-spirit coherence 119
Part 5: Transcend to an awakened consciousness 161
Part 6: Transfigure life, the universe and everything 197
Part 7: Living life on Earth now 239
Part 8: Epilogue 243

Acknowledgments 247

Important note:
Language of Spirit or 'One'

Throughout the pages of this book, a new language of spirit or 'One' has been used and incorporated to enable the reader to realise a new way of perceiving, thinking, feeling, living and being in the world today.

The Sapir-Whorf hypothesis of linguistic relativity states that the language One speaks influences, limits and determines how One sees or perceives One's world and the universe. This book is written in an English 'spiritual language style', which uses the term 'One'. It reflects a non-dimensional and non-linear view of space–time. Every spiritual thought takes the form beginning with or inclusive of 'One', where 'One' is spirit, soul or cosmic consciousness.

'One' is an inclusive term referring to the spirit, soul, cosmic consciousness, Source, the Creator, God, Allah or Divine Supreme Being. It has been written in this way to reflect an intimate conversation between the spiritual Source for all things in the universe and One's spirit.

The terms 'I', 'you' and 'your' have been deliberately omitted in order to provide greater clarity, spiritual unity and global inclusiveness. This distinction is key and fundamental in shifting One's mindful perception to a more profound inner knowing and divine sense of oneness within One's spirit or Being. It is about intentionally and purposely co-creating a space with 'no self' to know oneself. To undertake One's ultimate spiritual journey in this life, it is best to remove oneself from the equation of One's life.

Where there is no 'I', there can be only 'One'. Where there is no 'You', there can be only 'One'. In the absence of 'I', 'me', 'mine', 'you' or 'your', there is only ever One's divine spirit, soul or cosmic consciousness. This is One's eternal presence in the universe. One has co-created this new language and the opportunity to inspire One's way of living and being through One's realisation and awakening of One's spiritual truth – here and now. Know that there is no space or distance between oneself and One's spirit. When One looks inwards, One will know One's inner way and direction in life.

There has never been a more perfect moment in One's life to journey deeply within oneself and awaken to One's own divine existence and living reality on Earth. All that ever was and will ever be in the universe is present within One's infinite divine presence 'Now'. Wherever One goes on planet Earth, or in any other part of the known universe, One is already home — Be Here Now.

Useful terms

Bright
An enlightened awake spiritual sentient Being.

co-existence theory of the universe
Where all dimensional matter-energy (altered consciousness) and non-dimensional states (consciousness) or field-states co-exist relative to each other. A theory of everything that describes the coherence of all separate theories into a single theory of co-existence within the universe. It is a theory that gives rise to a singularity of infinite existence in the universe.

Declaration of Freedom
The *Declaration of Freedom* is a belief system that affirms the inherent and inalienable right of all sentient Beings to be free. It states that all Beings, including humans, possess infinite potential and immeasurable power to co-create themselves and manifest any reality in the universe. It asserts that all beings are imbued with certain states of aligned consciousness, including inner knowing, awareness, oneness, joy, free will, peace, and presence, which are bestowed upon One by Source Consciousness.

The *Declaration of Freedom* emphasises that all human beings have the inherent right to be born free, live free and enjoy all the universal freedoms as citizens of Earth. These freedoms are not to be infringed upon by any external authority or institution and should exist in perpetuity for all future generations and Beings of the universe.

Declaration of Spirit

The *Declaration of Spirit* is a belief system that asserts the spiritual nature of human beings and One's purpose on Earth. It states that human beings are not merely physical beings but are instead spirit, soul, or cosmic consciousness hosting a human form or biological mind–body avatar.

In addition, the *Declaration of Spirit* declares that as a spiritual Being, One possesses seven distinct states of consciousness: knowing, awareness, oneness, joy, free will, peace, and presence, which are innate to every spirit. It emphasises that as a spiritual Being One is immortal, eternal, and infinite, and One's presence on Earth is not here by chance but by choice.

The *Declaration of Spirit* highlights the importance of radiating love, light and oneness to the world, honouring One's spirit and all other sentient Beings and aligning oneself with the synchronicity of the universe. It also stresses the importance of raising the conscious vibration of humanity to a higher state of existence in the galaxy by mindfully, intentionally and consciously manifesting a new reality through an individual paradigm shift within oneself.

Finally, the *Declaration of Spirit* envisions the conscious evolution of all humans towards a new interstellar spiritually united Type 1 civilisation on Earth. A world that is safe, free and co-created by all human beings believing and acting in synchronicity and harmony with 'the way' of the universe.

egosite

A person who has, holds or acts with an egoic parasitic intention, habit or behaviour to infect and feed off the spirit, soul, or cosmic consciousness energy of other living human beings for nefarious, unkind or self-serving purposes.

futurition

The act or process of introducing the spiritual consciousness of One's potential future self to One's present self. The state or condition of being aware of and connected to One's future potential. The study or contemplation of One's future spiritual evolution and potential.

global awakening process
A worldwide event whereby human beings voluntarily enter into and undergo a self-realisation and self-awakening journey of inner enlightenment to rise above individual egoic cultural and social programming by raising to a higher level of individual and collective spiritual consciousness on the planet.

global spiritual harmonic synergy
An inner state of interconnectedness and resonance among individuals, groups and the planet as a whole in which there is a shared sense of purpose, understanding and alignment with higher spiritual principles. It implies that when people are in harmony with themselves, with each other, and with the world around them, they can create a positive, uplifting energy that resonates throughout the globe. This energy can help to foster greater peace, compassion and understanding among all people, and promote a more sustainable and harmonious relationship between humanity and the natural world.

human coherent synergy
The idea that when people come together in a collaborative effort, they can achieve a level of unity and coherence that allows them to work more effectively towards a shared goal. This involves not only working together towards a common objective, but also aligning individual perspectives and values to create a cohesive vision that will enable people to manifest a new alternate reality and future now.

infinite state theory of spiritual consciousness
A way of predicting the probabilities of a sentient Being existing in one or all seven infinite states of consciousness. As a sentient Being of multi-non-dimensional conscious states, One exists in a single state and all states simultaneously (i.e. the eighth state). Until a particular state of spiritual consciousness is aligned within a sentient Being, One exists as an expression of any, multiple or all states of consciousness at the same time.

insanity
Being a sane person who tries repeatedly to 'fit' into a world where most people's minds are operating a stream of egoic unconscious mindless memes or thoughts.

lifernity
The concept of infinite existence, encompassing both the temporal nature of life and the eternal nature of the soul/spirit. One might say, 'The ultimate goal of spiritual consciousness is to attain a state of lifernity, where the individual transcends the limitations of time and space, and exists in a state of eternal harmony with the universe.'

This concept can apply to humans and One's spiritual evolution, as people strive to connect with One's true nature and attain a sense of purpose and fulfilment beyond the limited scope of One's human mortal lives. It can also apply to the broader context of spirituality and the interconnectedness of all Beings on the planet, as we recognise our shared journey towards an infinite existence.

light hole
A state of non-dimensional existence having an infinite presence of source consciousness so intense that all spiritual consciousness is drawn to it.

meme
An element of a culture or system of behaviour passed from one individual to another by imitation or other non-genetic means. Also an image, video or piece of text, typically humorous in nature, that is copied and spread rapidly by internet users, often with slight variations.

planetary citizenship
The position or status of being a citizen of a particular planet such as Earth or Mars.

reactive fear response
The automatic reaction of a human mind and body to a perceived threat or danger. It is a natural survival mechanism that prepares a human being to fight, flee or freeze in response to a potentially dangerous or life-threatening situation. This response is often characterised by the onset of physical changes such as increased heart rate, rapid breathing, sweating and heightened alertness, which help humans to avoid or react quickly and effectively to potential threats.

sacred space
An embodied emptiness by a particular individual within One's mind–body–spirit, holding a great respect, openness and alignment to co-create a new manifested reality or experience.

self-organising theory
The capacity of a system to change itself by creating new structures, adding new negative and positive feedback loops, promoting new information flows and making new rules. It is a process where the organisation (constraint, redundancy) of a system spontaneously increases, without this increase being controlled by the environment or an encompassing or otherwise external system.

seven key states of consciousness
Knowing, awareness, oneness, joy, free will, peace and presence.

seven key virtues
Compassion, helpfulness, acceptance, generosity, simplicity, patience and openness.

sol
A solar day on Earth. The interval between two successive returns of the Sun to the same meridian (sundial time) as seen by an observer on Earth.

spironergy
The state of being in harmony with One's spiritual consciousness and the energy of the universe, leading to a heightened sense of potential and power. The belief in the ability to access and use spiritual energy for personal growth and transformation. The study or practice of using spiritual energy for physical and emotional healing, manifestation and spiritual evolution.

statum intuitanics
The state-based knowing, sensing or understanding by intuition and/or intuitive spiritual intelligence.

spiritual entanglement
A phenomenon where source consciousness is present in such a way that the individual spiritual states of consciousness exist independently until aligned, and the act of conscious alignment of one influences that of the other, even when at a distance from each other in space–time within the universe.

spiritual singularity
A state of non-dimensional conscious reality where states of consciousness exist in infinite or endless beingness.

spiritual sovereignty
A state of self-awareness and self-realisation about One's true spiritual nature as a divine spirit who has infinite existence in the universe and takes full self-responsibility for One's life. The act of freely declaring 'One is Spirit', 'One is Free Now'.

the awakening
A spiritual evolutionary process that affects all human beings by raising the vibrational energy of individuals and changing the living mindful state of consciousness to a higher level of existence on the planet.

the way
A term used in Buddhism or Zen teachings that, in its simplest definition, means an approach to life that flows in harmony and alignment with nature or the natural synergy of the universe in the present moment.

transhumanism
A philosophical and scientific movement that advocates the use of current and emerging technologies – such as genetic engineering, cryonics, artificial intelligence (AI), and nanotechnology – to augment human capabilities and improve the human condition. Transhumanists envision a future in which the responsible application of such technologies enables humans to slow, reverse or eliminate the aging process to achieve corresponding increases in human life spans and to enhance human cognitive and sensory capacities. The movement proposes that humans with augmented capabilities will evolve into an enhanced species that transcends humanity – the 'posthuman'.

Type 1 civilisation
The Kardashev scale categorises a civilisation's level of technological advancement based on the amount of energy it can use:
- a Type 1 civilisation can use and store all of the energy available on its planet
- a Type 2 civilisation can use and control energy at the scale of its planetary system
- a Type 3 civilisation can control energy at the scale of its entire host galaxy.

A Type 1 civilisation can harness all the energy that is available from a neighbouring star, gathering and storing it to meet the energy demands and needs of the population.

wellship

Wellship can be described as a type of bond or connection between two or more individuals that prioritises the overall health and wellbeing of all parties involved. It is a relationship that is centred on fostering the physical, mental, emotional and spiritual wellness of each individual, as well as the group as a whole. By focusing on enhancing and maintaining the holistic wellness of each person, wellship aims to create a supportive and nurturing environment that benefits everyone involved.

Introduction

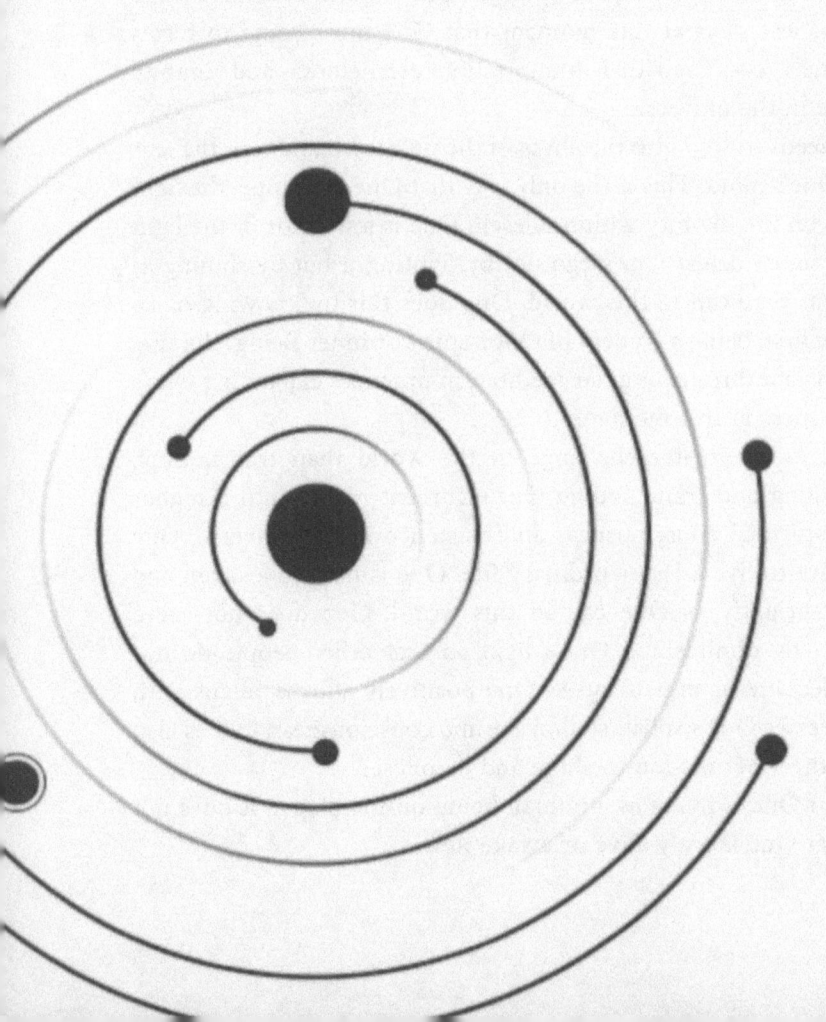

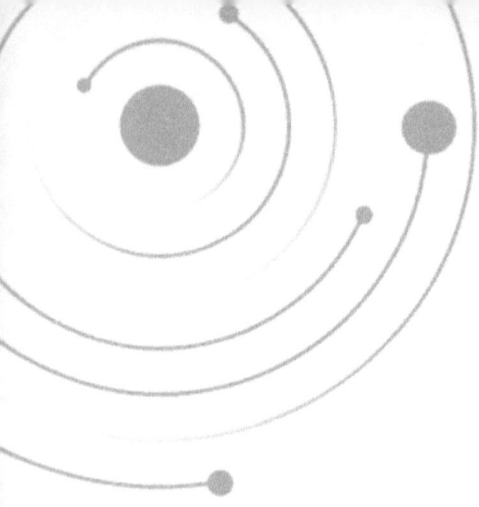

There are many people in the world who seek a spiritual path and way of life where One is able to free oneself from One's own ego without ever having to face oneself. This is an impossible task. In truth, everyone must look honestly into the mirror of self-reflection at the very deepest sense of One's spirit, soul or cosmic consciousness. It is at this moment that One must come to terms with One's own spiritual immortality, eternalness and infinite existence in the universe.

One needs to step into the abyss of the unknown and face the fear within One's mind. This is the only way that One can shine 'the light of truth' on the divinity within oneself. One is a warrior of the light and One must defeat One's ego not by fighting it but by shining as brightly as One can in this world. One does this by knowing of its existence first, being a student of One's spirit or inner Being, aligning to it daily and through regular meditation practices expanding One's consciousness at this moment.

There is no greater challenge in the world than transmuting, transforming and transcending One's current reality into a higher level of spiritual consciousness and existence in the universe. One is not here to live a lesser ordinary life. One is here to awaken and shine as brightly as One can in this world. One does not serve humanity by diminishing One's light so that other people do not feel inadequate or unworthy. As One positively affirms, aligns with and expresses One's spirit, soul or cosmic consciousness, One is also giving others permission to shine and be oneself.

Even if One is living as a human being on the planet, it does not mean that One is truly alive or awake now.

It can take a long time to break One's own human sociocultural programming because it has been uploaded and reinforced over decades. The neural pathways within One's brain are not all hard-wired into One's human living operating system. The good news is that, given the brain's neuroplasticity, it can be rewired and new pathways can be created. One's living operating system or LOS can be upgraded to a new and more spiritually conscious version of existence.

Society does a good job at building up false truths, fake personalities and fabricated identities. Seeing through the illusion which One has created within One's own mind will be One of the hardest life goals One will ever have to achieve. There is no greater spiritual quest than inside oneself. To evolve, One will need to transmute, transform and transcend One's human-based centric reality to a higher level of spiritual existence in this world. Especially when One has built a life and living purpose on that which One believes to be true and real.

Current so-called 'modern' societies and cultures openly give people false hope and promote the fiction that One is a human being. It implies that One is therefore important above all other species on Earth and interstellar visitors in the galaxy. This human-centric worldview is extremely narrow, very limited, particularly uninformed as well as completely short-sighted. One has been mistakenly led to the idea that One's egoic mind is the driver for all things and the centre of One's existence in the world and universe.

The paradigm for a new existence is all about changing from the doctrine of 'I think, therefore I am' to 'One exists – so One is.'

Whatever One's mind has been taught, trained and tutored in to educate oneself over the course of One's life will need to change. One needs to understand that most of the information has only been to inform One's mind and reinforce the status-quo of egoic thinking and belief systems in the world. All egoic thoughts have only been there to give egoic ideas, concepts and actions meaning at the expense of One's spirit, soul or cosmic consciousness.

> **One's free will is an integral part of One's spiritual identity and divine sovereignty. It exists in perpetuity.**

It is everything to anyone who believes in oneself. One's spirit is free. One's egoic mind is the prison from which One needs to escape and be all that One can be in this world. Cultures, communities and societies put too much needless pressure on people to conform, comply and live a conditioned way of thinking and living. When One discovers who One truly is and was meant to be in life, it will create a ripple of realisation within oneself that will lead to One's own awakening and a dramatic shift in One's way of life on the planet. However, people's own egos and most of society will still choose to resist change and fight it to the very end.

Poor living is largely a result of a lack of prosperity thinking, not the lived experience of poverty itself. The same can also be said about an egoic lifestyle – it is a lack of awareness of One's spirit, soul or cosmic consciousness, not the lived experience of ego itself. A person who hides behind the mask of ego will always live a significantly more diminished life. This type of person will always be a prisoner of One's own egoic beliefs, thought patterns, habits, behaviours and actions.

When One finally breaks free of One's mental conditioning, One is so grateful to finally realise One's place, purpose and destiny now. It is like a dark cloud has been lifted or chains have been removed, allowing One to finally be free. One is truly in awe of One's inner change and One can celebrate being a sentient Being of the universe. One has the opportunity to be so much more. One can radiate One's light upon the world and give truly of oneself after making the decision to be free of One's ego. But it takes time, effort and commitment to stay in alignment with One's spirit. Being kind, caring and compassionate as well as virtuous on a daily basis requires intentional mindful practices and a commitment to expressing it in the moment when it arises. After all, to manifest One's future reality means being truly present now.

Living an intentional spiritual-centric life and lifestyle requires One to first accept that One is a spiritual Being having a human experience and not a human being having a spiritual experience. This is another important paradigm shift which One needs to embrace and come to terms with as soon as possible.

This book has been written in a user-friendly way to guide One's spiritual evolution and divine existence on Earth. Each of the eight parts focus on specific elements and certain aspects of the evolutionary process:

Structure of this book

Part 1: Welcome to Earth

Part 2: Spirit, soul or cosmic consciousness

Part 3: Transmute One's spiritual existence

Part 4: Transform One's mind-body-spirit coherence

Part 5: Transcend to an awakened consciousness

Part 6: Transfigure life, the universe and everything

Part 7: Living life on Earth now

Part 8: Epilogue

Each part delves into a particular topic and dives deep into exploring the themes within it. This is done through general discussion as well as answering specific questions in response to life, the universe and everything now.

Use each part of this book to reflect, review and reveal answers to questions that One may have about spiritually evolving on the planet. While it is best to flow from Part 1 to Part 8, it is not necessary. One may wish to skip about and reread various parts of the book to embed some of the key learnings, teachings and pointings.

In truth, there is no right or wrong way to evolve as a sentient Being on Earth, there is only 'the way' in synchronicity with the universe. What works for oneself or is the best medicine with respect to this process can only be truly known when One explores it for oneself. Personal experience is the great teacher of life, especially if One is open and honest enough to listen and learn.

Use this book as a guide to find One's way to the truth and journey along an inner path to evolve as a spiritual Being on Earth. It is time to become an awakened 'Bright' in the universe now.

Believing in the conscious truth of the universe is an act of spiritual evolution

EVOLVE

Transmute · Transform · Transcend

One's guide to spiritual evolution in the Universe

PART ONE

Welcome to Earth

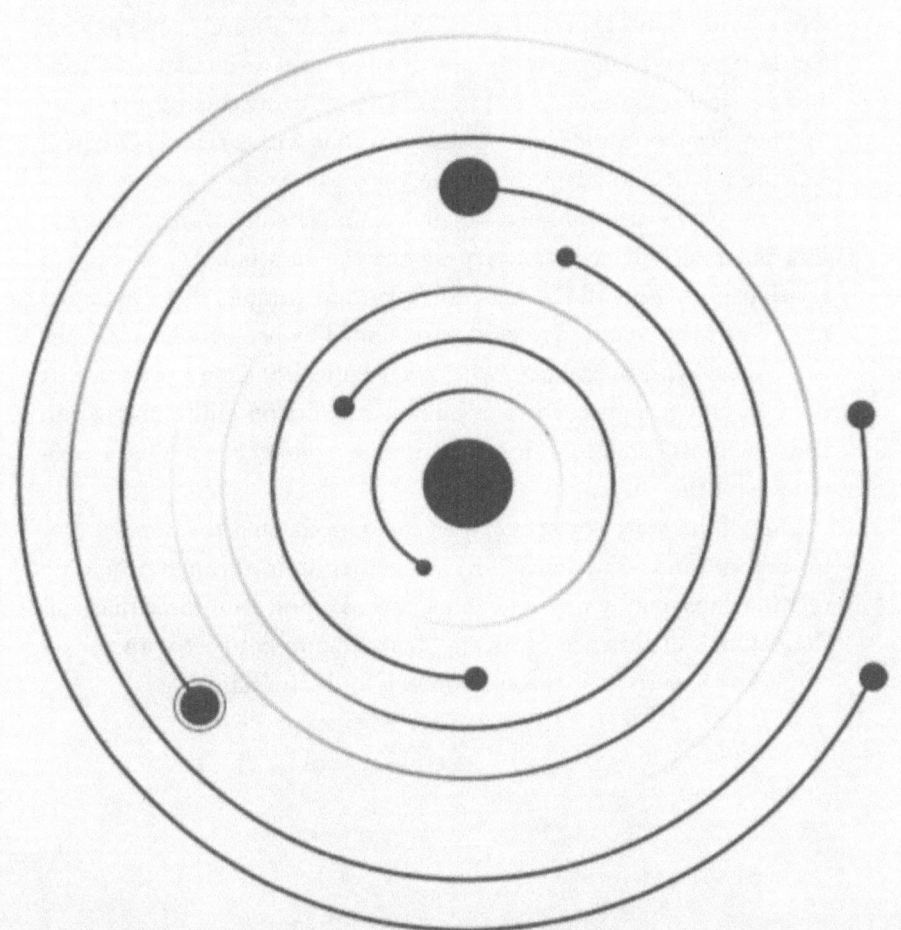

First day on Earth

As a spiritual Being, arriving on Earth for the first time can be an exciting and overwhelming experience. One may feel disoriented and curious about living in this new world, on this new planet, with its diverse cultures, languages and landscapes.

One thing to expect is a sense of 3D density and physicality that One may not have experienced before. One's body and thoughts may feel heavier and One may be more vulnerable to human emotions and physical sensations. It can be a challenge to successfully navigate this new level of mind–body physicality, but with practice, One will learn to adjust and adapt over time.

With One's new human form (male, female, transgender or non-binary), One will also experience the rich tapestry of human relationships, with all the joys, sorrows, and complexities contained in it. One may even find oneself surrounded by people who are eager to connect with oneself, or who are sceptical of One's presence. It is important to approach each human interaction with compassion and openness, and to remember that everyone is on One's own unique journey here.

One of the most powerful experiences on Earth is the opportunity to express and experience love. Whether it is through romantic relationships, family or friendships, love is a powerful force that will shape One's experience on Earth. Take time to connect with others and allow love to flow through oneself and One's life.

Love is the bridge between you and everything.
Rumi

It can also be helpful to cultivate a spiritual practice that supports One's connection to the divine and helps One navigate the ups and downs of life on Earth. This can take many forms, such as meditation, yoga, or journaling, and will help One stay centred and grounded when navigating this new world.

As One begins One's journey on Earth, know that One is not alone. There are many spiritual Beings like oneself who have come before, and who are here now to support One. Trust in One's journey and know that everything One experiences is helping One to grow and evolve.

Only through One's spirit can One truly experience the infinite love, peace and divinity of the universe.

Congratulate oneself for choosing Earth as One's entry point into the third dimension or 3D. As part of One's conscious spiritual awareness, One intuitively knows that One is here now on 'starship Earth', orbiting the sun in this solar system. It is part of One's unending journey travelling across the Milky Way galaxy in this celestial sector of the universe.

Before One starts, know that One has an important life purpose, mission and goal. One's human life is limited here on Earth and so One needs to make the most of it in every way possible. One's spiritual journey of divine evolution flows effortlessly forward into the future now. A continuum of infinite beingness within this moment that is spiritually expressed through One's human form. Take a deep breath and realise that One is a spiritual traveller and an integral part of the universe.

One already knows with great certainty One's spiritual vision in this life, One is committed to evolving and assisting others to align with One's own spirit, soul or cosmic consciousness on this planet. One has a mission to help all humans to raise the vibration of spiritual consciousness within oneself, improving the prosperity, abundance and wakefulness of humanity on Earth. One is here to benefit the people of this world to collectively evolve into a new spiritual age of 'awakened consciousness' or 'spiritual enlightenment'. It is a shared responsibility that everyone takes One's cosmic place amongst the other interstellar spiritually united Type 1 civilisations in this galaxy.

One is finally here now on Earth. It is cause for a special greeting to welcome One as a new spiritual traveller to One's new host family, kin, community, First Nation and host human body (male, female, transgender or non-binary). The universe has an incredibly unique way of doing things that will make this the greatest spiritual experience of One's current life, but it will require a commitment to align, courage to change and an effort to evolve. Know that One cannot change in the absence of pain and growth. It is a natural consequence of One's human form that One will accept, alter and adapt. This is all an integral part of transmuting, transforming and transcending One's human life experiences.

This book was written from the perspective of someone who has been exactly where One is now and who seeks to discover the truth and way of spiritual evolution as easily and effortlessly as possible in this life.

A path that is free of ego and the white noise of sociocultural programming of the past. A way to know One's inner spirit and not conform to the global illusion of reality in the world. A process that is grounded in the conscious belief that One is spirit and here to become awake for the purposes of spiritual evolution in the universe. A journey that is outlined for One to mindfully and virtuously express One's daily thoughts, behaviours, habits, speech and actions.

Know that on One's first day on Earth, when One takes One's first breath, One is free. One is free of ego. One is uniquely spirit with a human form or Earthly avatar. One is pure and One is truly blessed with infinite potential in this life. One is incredibly powerful beyond measure. One is a beautiful Being of light, love and divine oneness. One is truly special – just believe and it will be so. One is and has always been an integral part of the universe.

What comes next … will all be revealed to One in this life. At the right time, in the right way and with the right people. Free One's mind and allow oneself to be guided by One's spirit and the universe now.

Spiritual facts that matter

There is no escaping or denying the truth that One is spirit, soul or cosmic consciousness. Since the dawning of humanity on Earth and the earliest days of spiritual awareness, it has been incredibly important to realise that One is a free spirit of the universe. One has within oneself the freedom to shape and influence One's spiritual journey and manifest One's human experiences in the world. One has the ability to co-create the reality that One seeks and chooses to believe in now. So, to effectively navigate a spiritual path and evolve on Earth, One must know, embrace and accept One's spirit, soul or cosmic consciousness.

In knowing spirit at a deep, personal and intimate level, One must first be aware of the seven truths about One that are the starting point for One's spiritual journey here on Earth.

The seven truths of 'One' or spirit

1. One is and will always be an eternal, immortal, and infinite spiritual Being.
2. One is a free spirit, existing in an endless continuum of infinite beingness beyond space and time (non-dimensional multi-state-based existence).
3. One is oneness, nameless, formless, timeless, shapeless, sexless, egoless, fearless, selfless, and pure cosmic consciousness itself.
4. One exists in any or all seven states of divine consciousness (knowing, awareness, oneness, joy, free will, peace, and presence) at any given moment in the universe.
5. One is spirit, soul or cosmic consciousness and host to One's human (mind–body) form and manifested experiences in the universe.
6. One co-exists in a divine synergy of pure consciousness (spirit) and altered consciousness (mind–body).
7. One is here now to awaken to One's spiritual reality and be present at this moment as a sentient Being of the universe to exist, express and experience conscious mindful living and being now as part of One's journey of infinite existence.

In understanding these seven truths, One must also be aware of what is not true about One.

- One is **not** One's mind or any thought that has or will ever be created within it.
- One is **not** One's body regardless of its shape, colour, ethnicity, race, size, age, height, weight, gender, appearance by virtue of its DNA code or how it is clothed, modified or presented to the world in which One lives.

- One is **not** One's partnership/parenting/family/sibling/kinship role or relationship even though it may have been and continue to be integral to the socioeconomic-cultural development, eco-enviro conditioning, moral/ethical shaping and engagement of oneself on a daily basis.
- One is **not** One's place or position in society even if One has been elevated to it through natural birth, personal achievement or specific circumstances, chance, luck, longevity, deeds, fame, celebrity status, popularity, election, social pursuits, acknowledgments or group accolades.
- One is **not** One's achievements even if One has spent a lifetime working with people to create a positive change or improve the world One lives in through simple acts of care, kindness and compassion or through life-changing inventions, incredible discoveries, groundbreaking research or perhaps inspiring new innovations.
- One is **without** religion, belief, ideology, gender, sexuality, race, culture, age and nationality.
- One is **without** concern, worry, anxiety, disease, illness or fear.
- One is **without** attachment, resistance and judgement of any and all things in the universe too.

If One is none of these things associated with human activity or One's human form, One may very well ask the question – who is One?

When One arrived on Earth, One was already imbued with seven states of cosmic consciousness:

> **The seven states of cosmic consciousness**
> 1. Knowing
> 2. Awareness
> 3. Oneness
> 4. Joy
> 5. Free will
> 6. Peace
> 7. Presence

There is also an eighth state, which is all states in unity or a whole-of-consciousness state of existence.

This is the norm, in the universe or at most the starting point for undertaking One's spiritual journey on Earth. It has always been this way and will continue to be this way in the future. One needs to be grateful for One's spiritual existence in this dimensional world and thank those people who are integral to the survival of One's mind–body from an early age. Before the time of One's birth, One is pure consciousness. After the time of One's birth, One is still pure consciousness. This is where it all begins for spirits choosing to come to Earth and live in this world. One is free and has free will to make One's own decisions about what One uploads into One's mind or human operating system and other choices in life.

One is here to awaken – now.

When One starts One's new spiritual journey and life on Earth, One is without the memories of One's previous incarnations here and past lives on other worlds in the galaxy or universe. One is essentially mentally free of One's lived history, which is a good thing, as One is able to hit the reset button and begin again. One is not encumbered by One's past successes or failures. One's existence in this new space–time continuum is a fantastic opportunity to co-create oneself and make great things happen. With One's new human form (male, female, transgender or non-binary), One can focus on important key tasks, missions and goals. This is great because One can live a new life, experience new things and become a new person or human avatar. However, before One can really enjoy all life has to offer, One must first realise two important fundamental truths about One's existence on Earth. To make this new life truly meaningful and purposeful, One must become aware of and realise two keystone messages of critical divine importance.

> **Keystone messages**
>
> 1   One is spirit, soul or cosmic consciousness.
> 2   One's purpose is to be 'awake' now.

When One finally becomes awake, it will change everything in One's life. One will not be able to look at One's life in the same way again. One's human form will become a 3D avatar and One's mind will be seen as the human living operating system that it is. One will recognise One's human identity as a false truth and reality as the illusion within the construct of the matrix of the world in which One is living now. One's mind–body will be akin to a human platform and operating software for living on Earth. But mostly, One will recognise One's infinite potential. In addition, One will also realise and directly experience One's loving-kindness and compassion to co-create oneself and manifest a new reality on Earth now.

The overarching idea that One needs to embrace is that all humans are in fact spiritual Beings with a soul or cosmic consciousness. There are seven truths about One's spirit that include being eternal and infinite, existing beyond space and time, and co-existing with One's human form. It is important to realise that One is not One's mind, body, relationships, achievements or attachments to things in the universe. One's spiritual existence is based on seven states of cosmic consciousness and One is free to shape One's journey and experiences. The goal is to awaken to One's spiritual reality and live a conscious and mindful life.

Welcome to life on Earth

Know that One brought oneself here for the purpose of being where One is now. One is here to experience a human life through a human form within the context of the living consciousness of One's infinite spiritual existence. One has within oneself all the interstellar wisdom that One requires to make this journey a living success. One also has the ability to 'tap into' or spiritually align with the infinite wisdom and cosmic energy of the universe too.

Know that One is a sentient Being of the universe with infinite potential and powers beyond measure. One can change One's life and so too the trajectory of people living on the planet. One's destiny is not determined by where One lives on the planet or the culture in which One was raised. One has the potential to transmute, transform and transcend every aspect of One's human conditioning and operating system. One can co-create the change that One seeks in this world to benefit all of humanity.

Let's be very clear. One did not come to Earth to play the game of ego or to subscribe to the illusion of material reality that is commonly held by most humans today. One is here for a higher purpose and mission to co-create the best version of oneself, spiritually evolve and raise the consciousness of humanity to a higher level of existence in the galaxy.

Even though One is an independent spirit, soul or cosmic consciousness, One exists within an ocean of infinite consciousness in the universe.

> **One is connected to everything and everything is connected to One.**

All Beings in the universe are spiritually entangled with other Beings – some more so than others. This is simply part of the fabric of non-dimensional beingness in which all sentient Beings exist.

Knowing One's place in the universe is great for maintaining a sense of One's higher self. It also assists with moving through the predictable and repeatable egoic human landscape in the world. When One realises this, One may feel great discomfort and misalignment to the control, conformity and certainty of the behavioural thought conditioning of the society in which One was raised and continues to live in now.

As One realises the extent to which egoic programming of people's human lives and living operating systems has pervaded every aspect of modern society, One will begin to see how it influences the majority of global decision-makers to support the continuation of greed, control, power, separation, conflict, violence, economic slavery, hate and bias toward an egoic construct to manipulate people's lives. There is an ongoing perpetual denial of spiritual existence on the planet. An ongoing system of economic slavery to maintain a mindless mass that makes it easier to control large groups of people from across the world. This is why the elites, governments, military, sanctioned covert groups and global organisations rely on it so heavily to suppress spiritual awakening and spiritual evolution on the planet.

But things are changing on Earth and people are beginning to wake up to One's divine existence in the universe. People are realising that the old ways of egoic living are out of date and no longer serve the good of humanity. Many are seeking a new reality to experience a better way of working, living, playing and being. There is a growing collective spiritual voice that is aligning to manifest a new Earth. One is committed to this global awakening and future reality now. One has been going out of One's way to promote this shift in consciousness and thinking to everyday intelligent, innovative, gifted, brilliant, inquisitive and curious people on Earth. Sharing this realisation, One aims to raise the vibration of 1 per cent of people on the planet as the tipping point so it changes the spiritual existence of all the remaining 99 per cent in favour of operating at One's higher level of spiritual consciousness.

The world requires spiritual innovators, soul ambassadors and consciousness advocates to manifest a new reality on Earth now. It is about co-creating a paradigm shift in each and every human being living in the world. This intention is to purposely enable a future where One can awake and be the sentient Being that One is meant to be in this galaxy. It is a call to spiritual action to enable and inspire an environment where people's spirits will be honoured, nurtured and thrive from the first day on Earth. This is why One is committed to creating a spiritual awareness within One and all of humanity.

One understands that, at present, the entire world has no collective governance or collective spiritual voice. In the absence of any global wisdom, shared responsibility or human management, nobody is 'held accountable' to anybody else for One's actions. International agreements between governments are made on the basis of what is good for One's own nation-state and not the good of the people on the planet. This is a prime example of egoic thinking in practice. It demonstrates a lack of planetary leadership and sociocultural stewardship which permeates from the highest levels of government to state governments, local governments and national institutions. Fabricated forces and false truths are in play around the world that promote an egoic agenda of greed over generosity, profits over people, economic slavery over self-sufficiency, and corruption over kindness or compassion. This is why the world needs to remove this 'egoic cultural algorithm' from society altogether. The only way to do this is to delete or remove it from One's own mind or living operating system. The message is clear: do not let ego be One's manager in life. One is better than this. One is spirit. One has so much more to offer the world, galaxy and universe at this point in One's life. Know that One's life path and true destiny will be revealed as One navigates it from a divine place of spirit, soul or cosmic consciousness and not driven by ego.

As an interstellar Being of light, One has the capacity to navigate One's life in a positive direction, creating new opportunities and moving away from 'dark or negative energies'. One has inherent gifts, skills and the power to green-light innovative ideas and collaborative projects that will benefit the world. With One's inner voice and vision, One can imagine a brighter future and manifest this reality on Earth now. Never underestimate the divine power that One has to change oneself and the world for the better. Although things may seem complicated and chaotic around the world, remember that One is not alone. One is part of the interconnected cosmic force for good in the galaxy. Remove all barriers in One's mind, as well as between oneself and other humans, to enable things to work. Be open to everyone and inclusive of all. Many people will say that 'the vision cannot be achieved' or 'it is too big and unrealistic' to be accomplished. But know that there is no statement that has any weight when compared with the aligned vibration of a new world on Earth. There is no red tape stopping One from figuring out for oneself the right path, the right way and working with the right people to make the vision a reality. One is an indomitable spirit, and One has faith in a future where an interstellar spiritually united Type 1 civilisation exists on Earth. One may be thinking to oneself, 'Wow, this sounds like a lot of responsibility', and, to some extent, One may be right. But it is a shared responsibility, and One is a single drop of spirit in a powerful ocean of conscious existence. When divine spirits collectively align in vibrational harmony in and across the world, it enables and co-creates a paradigm shift in the space–time continuum for everyone. This change creates an opening for a new reality to be manifested. One will then be able to change the trajectory of humanity, allowing people to mindfully and spiritually navigate towards a new way of working, living, playing and being in the world.

The single most important thing that One will ever do in this world is believe in oneself and be awake now. Any time One is about to think, say or do anything, One needs to ask oneself this question: Does this enable a new future on Earth? In the future, others will ask: What did One do to invest, improve and co-create a better world? How did One's thoughts, spoken words and actions contribute to manifesting the future prosperity and abundance of all people on Earth, in particular, seven generations after One was alive?

> **Invest with intention.
> Act without expectation.**

Investing with intention refers to the deliberate and thoughtful process of putting One's resources, time and energy into something that aligns with One's human values, virtues and goals. This approach requires One to be mindful of One's actions, to understand the motivations behind them, and to make decisions that align with One's personal values, inner virtues, spiritual truths and life objectives.

Acting without expectation means that One is free from any attachment to the outcome of One's actions. One is not focused on what One will gain or lose; instead, One is focused on doing what is right and what aligns with One's individual values or 'spiritual truth'. This allows One to approach investing with a clear mind and reduces the stress that comes with trying to achieve specific outcomes.

Investing with intention and acting without expectation is a powerful combination that can help One to achieve One's aspirational goals and live a life that is fulfilling and meaningful. It allows One to focus on the process and enjoy the journey, not just the end result.

To invest with intention, start by setting clear achievable goals that aligns with One's values, virtues, truth and priorities. Consider clearly what One desires to achieve today, tomorrow or over this lifetime and why One seeks to achieve it. This will help One make informed and thoughtful investment decisions that align with One's vision for the future.

Acting without expectation means letting go of the attachment to the outcome of One's personal investments, such as time, energy and resources as well as mind–body–spirit. This can be difficult, but it is essential for reducing stress and allowing One to make the best decisions for One's future. When One acts without expectation, One is free to make decisions based on inner values, virtues, spirit and priorities, rather than being influenced by fear, greed or other emotions.

Investing with intention and acting without expectation is a potent fusion that can help One achieve One's future goals sooner and live a truly fulfilling life now. By focusing on the process and letting go of expectations, One can make spiritually informed and mindful decisions that align with who One truly is and how One chooses to express oneself in this life. Invest with intention, act without expectation and enjoy the journey on Earth.

Divine identity as a spiritual Being

Being aware of, understanding completely and truly knowing One's own divine identity as a spiritual Being is of utmost importance for personal growth and individual fulfilment. Understanding the spiritual aspect of One's Being helps everyone to connect with the divine within us all and to realise One's true potential. This knowledge provides a foundation for a more meaningful, fulfilling and contented spiritual life. It allows One to see beyond the physical 3D realm and experience the interconnectedness of all things in life.

As a spiritual Being, One can tap into One's inner wisdom and access the higher aspects of oneself. This understanding can help One to overcome obstacles and challenges, find peace and joy in the midst of chaos, and see One's life from a broader, more expansive, perspective. One can also gain a deeper understanding of the purpose of One's life and One's role in the world.

To truly know One's divine identity, One must first become aware of One's spiritual nature, consciousness or essence and understand that One is more than just a physical human being. One is made up of body, mind and spirit, and each aspect of oneself must be nurtured and developed in order to experience true contentment. This means taking the time to reflect on One's beliefs, values and virtues, to explore One's inner world, and to connect with the divine within One through meditation, prayer or other spiritual practices.

Another important aspect of understanding One's divine identity is recognising that One is part of a larger spiritual community. One is connected to all things and is part of a greater cosmic consciousness. This knowledge can bring a sense of peace and comfort, as One realises that One is not alone in the universe and that there is a greater purpose at work in everyone's lives.

The importance of being aware of, understanding completely and truly knowing one's own divine identity as a spiritual Being cannot be overstated. This knowledge provides a special foundation for One to be true to oneself and manifest a future reality that One so imagines or desires. It also helps One to experience the interconnectedness of all things. By nurturing and developing One's spiritual aspects within oneself, One can tap into One's inner wisdom, overcome obstacles and live a more meaningful, fulfilling and contented life.

The journey of self-awareness as a divine sentient Being begins the moment that One arrives and is born on Earth. Know that the majority of human identities or living operating systems within the people on the planet have been uploaded into One's mind in the first seven years of One's life. This occurred when One's child's brain was mostly in the theta mode and highly susceptible to suggestion. Theta brainwaves are One's gateway to learning, memory and intuition. The first seven years are considered the programming years of a human child. During this time, children will spend most of One's time in theta (4 to 8 cycles per second) and alpha (8 to 13 cycles per second) brainwave cycles, which is the same state that a person is in when they are in hypnosis or meditation.

This is the period that lays the foundation for One's human identity, personhood or residual self-image to be created, which is, in most cases, a false truth. Whatever One has been told as a child by One's parents, family, community and society in today's 'non-spiritual' world is a fabrication or scaffolding for the ego to exist. This is particularly relevant in modern Western societies and across the world. One's foundation identity or personhood in society is an artificial construct and will most likely be ego-centric unless it is purged from within oneself. This may come as a shock to most people who do not realise that One is not human – One is spirit, soul or cosmic consciousness. This is the truth of One's existence on Earth as a sentient Being of the universe.

The ego operating system within One's mind which has most likely been installed gradually over One's formative years has created the construct of One's human identity. It will say and do almost anything to deny its own existence, deinstallation or death. Most people on the planet do not realise that One has been walking around with this viral egoic operating system influencing every decision One has ever made in One's life. People will go to incredible lengths to protect, preserve and promote One's mind's egoic structures, beliefs and boundaries. Because One's mind believes it to be true – but it is not. Ego is only an artificial program or thought algorithm within One's mind that has been validated by One's friends, family, kin, community and the society in which One lives. Eventually after One awakes to the truth of being spirit, soul or cosmic consciousness, the ego dies within because One no longer identifies with it or believes in it as the source of truth for One's life.

The source of truth for One's existence in this world is One's inner spirit, not the false idea or social construct of who One thinks One is or was told to be by another person in life.

Like the lotus flower of awareness, One must open One's mind and realise the universal truth within One's spirit now. One's most single point of truth in the universe is One's divine identity, not the human avatar that One is walking around in from day to day.

It is a trick of the ego within One's mind to hide the 'real self' from One. But One's ego will only ever exist for however long that One believes in it. The issue, concern and worry is that the majority of people in current societies and social structures on the planet are designed to validate and reinforce ego while at the same time denying the existence of spirit within oneself.

Trillions of dollars are spent and invested each day to promote planetary-wide systems that maintain a collective illusion of separateness that corrupts people's perceptions of the world. The result of this creates and reinforces judgement of others, attachment to fear, drugs, money, illness, conflict and violence as well as resistance to change. There are global governance and monetary systems in place with the primary goal not to support One's personal wellbeing, enable positive wellships or improve the wellness of humanity on the planet. These systems co-exist to pervert, distort and manipulate people into believing in a vibration of greed, materialism, selfishness, hatred, animosity, adversarial engagement, political-corporate power and intergenerational economic slavery.

Most people have been systematically and institutionally brainwashed or programmed into believing in One's own ego and not in the greater good of the planet and the people living on it. Families, children and young people have been continually exposed to intergenerational conditioned thinking for so long that One is unable to realise the truth of One's divine identity and existence in the world today. But One has the power to transmute, transform and transcend One's living experiences on Earth. One can realise One's new inner journey of divine awareness and embrace it completely as a spiritual Being of the universe.

Whatever the world says One is, know that One is not. Whoever One was in the past, One is not this person today either. Whatever One did yesterday, One can co-create a better version of oneself in this present moment now. One can never fail at being spirit, soul or cosmic consciousness. Simply remove One's human avatar from the equation of One's life and start living as a Being of love, light and oneness. What One does now matters. What One creates today shapes the future reality for oneself and all of humanity. Release oneself for all One's past mistakes, mishaps and missed opportunities. Shift One's coherent mind–body–spirit energy into a higher vibrational level of existence on the planet. One is right on time to become the 'Bright' or awake Being that One is meant to be in this world.

Embrace this moment, accept this new life and live One's inner truth – as a sentient Being of the universe.

> **Within One is One's divine truth – within this truth exists One's spiritual identity and cosmic sovereignty.**

Believe and so it will be now.

Being an Interstellar Ambassador

Becoming an Interstellar Ambassador is important in this modern age because it promotes peaceful and cooperative relationships between different civilisations in the Milky Way galaxy, and it helps to ensure the long-term survival of humanity.

As humanity continues to explore space and search for established friendly extra-terrestrial life, it is likely that humanity may encounter other intelligent Beings who have developed distinct and unique cultures, beliefs, values and advanced technologies on One's home worlds. By becoming an Interstellar Ambassador, One can represent this planet and establish respectful communication with other civilisations, fostering mutual understanding, inner planetary trade or exchanges and peaceful interstellar cooperation.

Additionally, the study of other worlds and new planetary environments can help humans gain valuable knowledge and resources that can benefit Earth. Becoming an Interstellar Ambassador, therefore, not only promotes interstellar cooperation and understanding but also contributes to the advancement of human knowledge, spiritual evolution and the sustainable advancement of this world.

The world does not require more politicians, lawyers, billionaires or soldiers. It requires mindful healers, helpful citizens and hopeful people to change and manifest a new world on Earth. There is an overwhelming need on the planet for intergalactic innovators, ideas initiators and intelligent creators. As part of the 'awakening process' unfolding on Earth now, it will be necessary to co-create and manifest consciously awake Beings. These Beings will be interstellar ambassadors of spiritual consciousness, peace, prosperity and abundance for a new future reality on the planet and in the solar system.

Calling oneself an 'Interstellar Ambassador' is easy, but becoming an effective ambassador takes time, energy, commitment, work, meditation, cooperation, spiritual alignment and a successful win–win–win strategy to truly become One that is recognised and able to bring great value to all people living on Earth.

So, how does One become a successful Interstellar Ambassador? The first and most important step is to believe in oneself above all else and trust the process of the universe to reveal all as One requires it.

Seven tips to fast track One's success in life as an Interstellar Ambassador

Know Oneself, One's Spirit, Soul or Cosmic Consciousness

One does not need a university degree to know what is within oneself. One only requires the space and time to meditate in peace. One has the capacity within oneself to directly align with One's inner spirit anytime or anywhere in the world. Through the silence of meditation, One will be able to tap into the wisdom of the universe. In addition, it is in the 'spiritual state of knowing' where One will be guided to important decision points, paths and virtuous actions along 'the way' in life. Making One's presence known and reaching out to different people will become easy and effortless when done in a spiritually authentic and genuine way. Simply through intentional and mindful thinking, One will be able to make spiritual connections with people as One flows in harmony with the synchronicity of life itself in the universe.

 ### Desire to Be Open, Learn and Grow from Within

Develop an open and inquisitive mind to learn new things from the people that One is in contact with or working with in life. Use every opportunity to spiritually evolve into a Being of higher consciousness. Co-create a better version of oneself with whatever One is doing each and every day. Do not hesitate to ask people and seek others' opinions on how One becomes successful in life. Invite successful people to be One's mentors and inspiration to further motivate and drive One's spiritual success. 'Accept everything – reject nothing'.

 ### Be Adaptable, Flexible and Willing to Change

Make an effort to travel to different places, work with different people and serve others in this life. Invest in oneself to make this world a better place for all future generations. Be adaptable and flexible in different situations and environments One is working in now. Be lovingly kind and compassionate in responding to others or to any challenging situations. Make the best of every encounter with another spirit or human being in the world. See other people's spirit first and then adjust One's connection and alignment to raise the vibration to a higher level of consciousness. Attach to no person, idea, place or thing in this life. Be willing to change from the inside out.

Believe in a Vision for the Future

Have a vision, goals and a positive outlook on life. Always begin with the end in mind. 'Imagine it – Believe it – Manifest it' as One's living destiny. One's vision will give One motivation and confidence to become successful and reach for the stars. Do not worry if One stumbles or fails along the way, simply pick oneself up, dust oneself off and carry on achieving One's goal (it happens to everyone once in a while). Always create a positive outlook in life and believe in One's vision for the future as a manifested reality now. There are always other ways to achieve One's goal. Reassess, review and recommit oneself to the situation and simply move on with overflowing optimism and unconditional positivity.

Be Passionate, Positive and Proactive

Have passion, positivity and proactiveness for what One is doing in life. Allow One's spirit and passion to guide One's practice framework as this will bring positive energy and attract like-minded people. Being passionate also means that work becomes play – One's life will be a pleasure to live. Be positively persistent and personally proactive in achieving One's goals. Be all that One can be – choose life and live in the moment.

Learn from One's Mistakes and Continually Improve

No human being is perfect; everyone makes mistakes! Create the space to make sure One learns from One's mistakes. Do not live in the past. The present is the only place that One needs to be now. Adopt a continual quality improvement practice in all that One is committed to in life. Change any approach, behaviour or habit to become a better version of oneself. Learn from whatever One is doing or what One has done, absorb all constructive criticisms and improve One's attitudes, skills and abilities on a daily basis.

Stay True to One's Spiritual Beliefs and Never Give Up!

One is likely to encounter many things and experiences over the course of One's lifetime. It is only natural that One may like or dislike some things or people. On the other hand, One may find that some people have positive energy and others have negative energy. One is sure to fail along the way in achieving One's goals. Use these moments as a learning opportunity. Do not be hard on oneself. Remember to never give up on oneself – not now, not ever. Truly and honestly believe in One's spirit and the universe. Manifest everything in One's life through vibrational alignment and synergistic attraction. Things always change and change affects all things. It is not the level of effort that One needs to focus on, it is the continuity of effort One applies each and every day. Stay committed – eventually, sooner or later, One will achieve the outcome! Know that from little things, big things grow in life – be patient. Imagine living in a future where it is One's vision in this present moment. Be in vibrational alignment with a new reality and it will manifest now.

Spiritual call to action

Answering a spiritual call to action to evolve on planet Earth is important because it offers everyone the opportunity to tap into One's individual inner power and wisdom, connect with One's spirit, soul or cosmic consciousness and evolve into Beings of light, love and oneness. This journey towards a Type 1 civilisation will bring about a new era of peace, prosperity and evolution for all Beings on Earth and beyond.

The evolution of humanity towards a Type 1 civilisation, which is characterised by a harmonious and interconnected society that has advanced beyond the limitations of its planet, requires a spiritual call to action. The purpose of this call to action is to awaken individuals to One's spiritual truth and the power One possesses to shape One's living reality on a daily basis.

Answering this spiritual call to action involves developing a deeper understanding of One's self, as well as the universe and all that exists within it. This requires a shift in consciousness, away from materialism and towards spirituality. When individuals recognise the interconnectedness of all things, One can begin to tap into the infinite intelligence, energy and wisdom of the universe. This understanding enables One to work together in harmony, to heal the planet and bring about a new era of global peace, worldwide prosperity and abundance, and human spiritual evolution.

To manifest an interstellar spiritually based Type 1 civilisation on Earth, it is necessary to raise One's individual vibration and the collective consciousness of humanity. This can be done through practices such as meditation, mindfulness and acts of kindness and compassion. By focusing on these spiritual practices, individuals can tap into One's inner wisdom, connect with One's spirit, soul or cosmic consciousness and evolve into Beings of light, love and oneness.

The journey towards a Type 1 civilisation is not a solitary one, but a collective act of human coherent synergy and spiritual togetherness. As everyone works together and supports each other, a new world can be created based on love, compassion and unity.

This is the essence of a spiritually based Type 1 civilisation, and answering the call to action is an essential step in this journey.

Human coherent synergy is the idea that when people come together in a collaborative effort, they can achieve a level of unity and coherence that allows them to work more effectively towards a shared goal. This involves not only working together towards a common objective, but also aligning individual perspectives, values and virtues to create a cohesive vision.

The benefits of achieving a shared vision for humanity on Earth are numerous. First and foremost, it would provide a clear sense of direction and purpose for people across the globe, helping to guide decision-making and actions towards a common goal. This could lead to greater cooperation and collaboration across borders, and help address global challenges such as climate change, poverty and inequality.

Additionally, a shared vision could foster a sense of belonging and interconnectedness among people, which can promote empathy, understanding and compassion. This can lead to greater social cohesion and reduce conflict and division.

Overall, human coherent synergy and a shared vision for humanity on Earth can lead to greater unity, cooperation, and progress towards a more sustainable and equitable world for all.

To consciously and willingly move along this path towards the future now, One must realise that it is time to stop struggling, resisting inner change and experiencing ongoing personal pain and suffering. One's outdated and obsolete ego-centric thoughts, behaviours, beliefs, habits and actions no longer serve One. Know that One must finally say goodbye to One's old life. One must learn to reconfigure and transform One's old ways of thinking, speaking, living and doing, as well as One's old identity, to align with One's new reality, destiny and future. Let go of all negative thoughts, self-sabotaging habits, stressing about not being good enough and pretending to be someone that One is not. Realise that change is simply the synchronicity of the universe in action – One's job is to align One's mind–body–spirit to it.

Do not just take One's word for it. Look deeply inside oneself now. Admit to oneself that One's ego, egoic algorithm or conditioned thinking has failed One in life. Ego is a false prophet, fabricated mentor and – even worse – fake master. Ego makes great promises to deliver amazing outcomes but falls significantly short and underdelivers in most cases. The underlying belief of the majority of people currently living on the planet is that if only One works harder, smarter, faster and longer, One will achieve everything that One wants and desires in life. But guess what? This is totally and completely incorrect. More does not mean more quality of life. In most circumstances, it actually means less.

This is why it is so important to answer One's spiritual call to action. One must 'wake up' and spiritually evolve into a 'Bright' – an awake sentient Being of light, love and oneness in the galaxy.

Know that whatever One is seeking is already within oneself. It has been there since One arrived on Earth as spirit, soul or cosmic consciousness.

One's first lesson is free and here it is!

First lesson of life

Know that everything that One has done has been to bring oneself to this moment and point in time in One's life. But this will not be enough to get One where One needs to be to spiritually evolve. To take the next step in One's spiritual evolution will require One to do something different from what One has always done in the past. One will need to escape the gravitational pull of One's previous mental construct (psycho-sociocultural programming) and human avatar. This will free oneself to become awake and evolve into the sentient Being that One is meant to be in this life.

What this means is that in order to transcend mind-based dimensional thinking, One will need to upload a new awakened thought-stream of higher consciousness. One will also need to consciously shift to operate from a spiritual non-dimensional navigation system within oneself.

Know that One is unable to think One's way out of the issue, problem or concern using the same level of thinking that created the condition in the first place. One needs to break free of One's previous conditioned thinking, beliefs and processes using One's higher level of consciousness – this is the key to inner and outer freedom in One's life.

To completely change the trajectory of One's life and this planet, One must change oneself from the inside at this present moment now.

This may appear to be an impossible task, but it is not. One simply needs to breathe, let go and shift One's energy to a higher vibration. Relax and release all attachments. Surrender and align with 'the way'. Every obstacle in life is an opportunity to grow, change and transform One's thinking, beliefs, approach, attitude, habits and way in life. When One's mind is calm and centred in stillness, like a smooth pond of water, One will be able to see clearly into this present moment. One will also be able to peer into every other imaginable future reality that One can perceive. The universe will reveal what One needs to know and One will intuitively know what One needs in this moment too.

If life is not working out for One now, what has One got to lose?

It is time to get inspired to change One's life. In lieu of not finding a spiritual Mentor, Elder or Master to provide guidance, simply act with genuine, honourable and open intentions to journey along 'the way' in life. When One does this, it will make a real, positive difference to oneself and One's friends, family, kin, community, First Nation and the world.

One may now be thinking, 'This all sounds great but how does One make it happen? Where does One begin?' It is simple – just say 'Yes' and invite oneself to change in alignment with the synchronicity of the universe. Flow with life and the natural rhythm of living in harmony with spirit and Country (land, sea and sky).

Get inspired, get excited and get motivated to manifest a new reality on Earth where One is living life at a higher level of spiritual consciousness. Start a conversation with oneself first. Write One's thoughts down in a journal, start meditation or yoga classes or undertake solo meditation sessions at home, work or anywhere One is. Start with 5 to 10 minutes, then longer as One becomes more comfortable with the practice.

Know that One is an interstellar agent of conscious change (i.e. a consciousness creator) and has the capacity to manifest any reality or experience in the world. What One does today matters in life and shapes the future. Whether One realises it or not, One is a cosmic influencer of One's reality and life on the planet.

Let's do this now. Begin by reading the following statements out loud or silently within One's mind to change One's living vibrational energy in the universe. This will attract all that One seeks in direct proportion to a shift in One's harmonic living resonance or 'chi'.

Thank you, universe, for the opportunity to become aware, awake and change now.

One knowingly, willingly and openly says:

'Yes' to being spirit, soul or cosmic consciousness.

'Yes' to purging One's ego from One's mind completely.

'Yes' to being fully awake now.

'Yes' to being guided by spirit and the synchronicity of the universe to evolve into a Being of higher spiritual consciousness.

'Yes' to inner-outer change (mind–body–spirit) to evolve into a 'Bright'.

'Yes' to manifesting a new life, new thinking, new ways of working, living and being in the world.

'Yes' to a new interstellar spiritually united Type 1 civilisation on Earth.

'Yes' to believing wholeheartedly in this future reality and destiny.

'Yes' to this living future amongst the stars and experiencing life as One's higher spiritual self.

One says 'Yes', 'Yes', 'Yes' and invites the universe to support One now.

Mindful meditation moment

Create an inner sanctuary within One's mind and space in One's life to be still, silent and serene. Use this affirmation practice to align with One's spirit, soul and cosmic consciousness.

[repeat 3 times then move on to the next affirmation]

Breathe in and say to oneself: *One is spirit ...*

Hold for 4 seconds

Breathe out and say to oneself: *One is at peace ...*

Breathe in and say to oneself:
One is immortal, eternal and infinite ...

Hold for 4 seconds

Breathe out and say to oneself:
One is a divine light of the universe

Breathe in and say to oneself:
One is an indomitable spirit ...

Hold for 4 seconds

Breathe out and say to oneself:
One has infinite potential ...

Breathe in and say to oneself:
One is whole and worthy

Hold for 4 seconds

Breathe out and say to oneself:
One is special and unique ...

Breathe in and say to oneself:
One is powerful beyond measure

Hold for 4 seconds

Breathe out and say to oneself:
One is able to manifest any reality

Declaration of Spirit

The *Declaration of Spirit* is a powerful and important guide for humanity to evolve on Earth and create a new interstellar life. This declaration is significant because it reminds everyone that people are not just human beings, but also spiritual Beings with a deeper purpose. By recognising and embracing One's spiritual truth, nature or essence, One can tap into the infinite existence of all things in the universe to create a new reality for oneself and the world.

The seven distinct states of consciousness described in the declaration are essential for this evolution. These inner states – knowing, awareness, oneness, joy, free will, peace and presence – provide humankind with a deeper understanding of who One is and One's place in the universe. By accessing these states, One can tap into One's inner wisdom and raise One's vibration to a higher level of consciousness.

The *Declaration of Spirit* also reminds people on the planet that One is here on Earth by choice, not by chance. This means that One has a purpose. One is here to be awake and raise the conscious vibration of all humanity. One is a co-creator of One's reality, and it is through One's coherent (mind–body–spirit) thoughts and actions that One can manifest a new paradigm that supports the conscious evolution of all humans towards a new interstellar spiritually united Type 1 civilisation on Earth.

This declaration is relevant to humanity because it offers a roadmap for One's individual personal growth and collective spiritual evolution. By embracing One's spirit, spiritual truth, nature or essence and recognising One's place in the universe, everyone can work together to create a better world for oneself, others and future generations. This is the significance and relevance of the *Declaration of Spirit* to humanity and everyone's evolution on Earth.

In the end, it will bring about a new era of global peace, worldwide prosperity, planetary abundance and spiritual evolution for all Beings on Earth and beyond.

Declaration of Spirit

One is here by choice not by chance. One solemnly and sincerely declares that One is spirit, soul or cosmic consciousness, One is not human, One is only host to One's human form (male, female, transgender or non-binary) and One's spirit is imbued with seven distinct states of consciousness: knowing, awareness, oneness, joy, free will, peace and presence There is also an eighth state, which is all states in unity or a whole-of-consciousness state of existence.

One is immortal, eternal and infinite, One is at peace, One is worthy, One is whole and meant to be where One is now. One radiates One's love, light and oneness to the world. One honours One's spirit and all other sentient Beings. One is aligned to One's spirit and the synchronicity of the universe. One is here on Earth to be awake and raise the conscious vibration of all of humanity to a higher state of existence in the galaxy. One is safe, free and a co-creator of One's reality. One is mindfully, intentionally and consciously manifesting a new reality through a paradigm shift that will support the conscious evolution of all humans towards a new interstellar spiritually united Type 1 civilisation on Earth.

Copy the statement above, in full or in part, into a favourite notebook or onto a fresh, clean sheet of paper, and combine it with One's own words. Alternatively, choose the words or statements that most resonate with One's inner sense of spiritual identity and create a new, blended *Declaration of Spirit* to affirm One's belief in One's higher self. Sign and date it to signify One's commitment to the words.

IMPORTANT LEARNINGS, TEACHINGS AND POINTINGS

Key ways to being a sentient Being of the universe

01 Realise that One is only a host to One's human form (male, female, transgender or non-binary). One is spirit, soul or cosmic consciousness.

02 One is imbued with seven distinct states of consciousness: knowing, awareness, oneness, joy, free will, peace and presence. (There is also an eighth state, which is all states in unity or a whole-of-consciousness state of existence.)

03 One is here now on Earth to 'wake up' and raise the living consciousness of humanity to a higher level of existence in the galaxy. This is all integral to One's spiritual evolution in the universe. Only by purging, deconstructing or the death of One's ego from One's mind will One be free to manifest a new reality on Earth – an interstellar spiritually united Type 1 civilisation .

04 The source of truth for One's existence in this world is One's inner spirit, not the false idea or social construct that One thinks One is or was told to be by another person in life.

 The planet requires mindful healers, helpful citizens and hopeful people to change and manifest a new world on Earth. We need intergalactic innovators, ideas initiators and intelligent creators. As part of the 'awakening process' unfolding on Earth now, it will be necessary to co-create and manifest consciously awake Beings. It is time to be an interstellar ambassador of spiritual consciousness, peace, prosperity, and abundance for a new future reality on the planet and in the solar system.

 Know that One is an interstellar agent of conscious change with the capacity to manifest any reality or experience in the world.

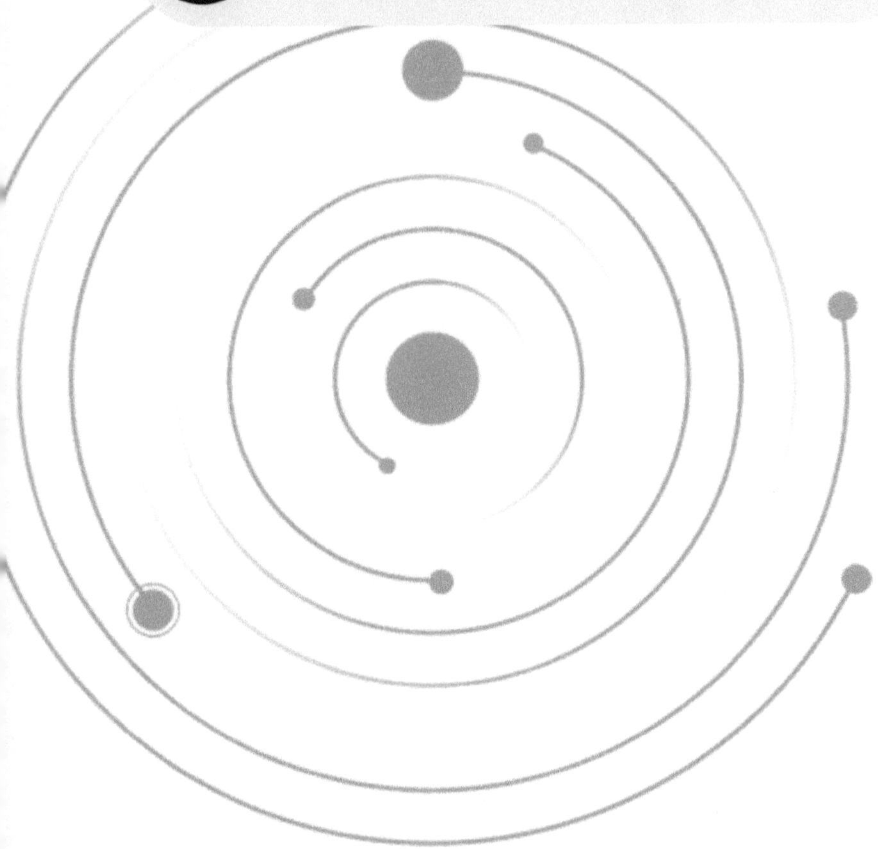

PART TWO

Spirit, soul or cosmic consciousness

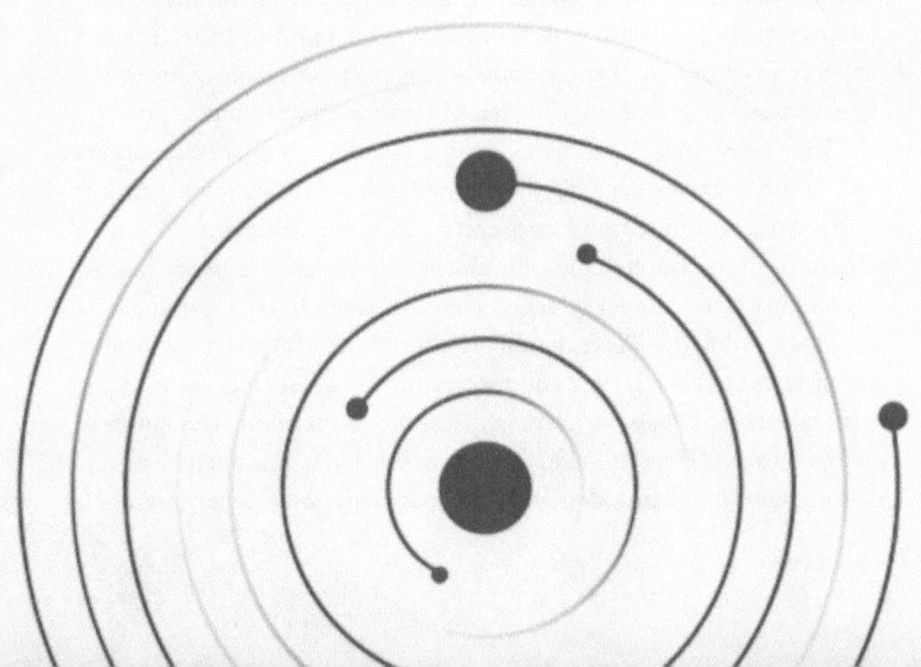

One is not alone

One has never been alone in the universe. This is the reality of One's existence as a sentient Being. Just because One is unable to meet, see, perceive or have an ongoing relationship with other interstellar Beings at this time, does not mean that they do not exist in this galaxy or in another part of the universe. It is nonsensical and species-biased to think that the universe, this galaxy, solar system and Earth was only created for humans. In a universe so vast, the potential for life to exist on other planets is a mathematical probability and divine certainty. Somewhere out there in space and time, other humanoid interstellar Beings exist that are thousands of years more consciously awake and technologically advanced than humans here on Earth today.

Substantial evidence already exists on Earth about interstellar Beings making contact with humans. At this point in time, it is not openly disclosed. It is intentionally and purposely hidden from the public and the world under a veil of secrecy and red tape.

Top secret black projects – unacknowledged special access programs – exist under highly guarded and protected joint ventures between government and corporate aerospace companies. Most of these projects are classified as 'above top secret'. They are funded through a black budget which is now estimated to be approximately 2.3 trillion dollars. These special unacknowledged projects are located in government black sites and research facilities, such as S4 near the dry lake bed of Papoose Lake, which is about 30 kilometres south of 'Area 51', near Groom Lake in Nevada. It is likely managed by covert teams within existing deniable secret structures of governments. It is also widely known that, as an Earth-based species, humans have been and are continuing to have contact and connection with more spiritually and technologically advanced Beings from other worlds in the galaxy.

The more One awakens, the more One becomes aware of other interstellar conscious intelligences in the galaxy. Know that One is not alone. One has never been alone in the universe. One is part of something greater, bigger and more magnificent than the average human mind can imagine.

The ego within One's mind will always strive to encourage One to think with limitations, believe in false truths, feel small, alone and insignificant. It is reassuring that One's spirit knows the truth of One's existence in the universe.

One's inner consciousness will always seek to reach out and expand in a way that touches other spiritual intelligence and harmonises with the divine Source of light in other sentient Beings in the universe. There is nothing so beautiful as when One aligns in spiritual harmony with another Being and shares the oneness of One's existence at that moment. This is such a powerful experience, as found when One is 'in love' and has lost of sense of self or ego and can only feel a unity of existence that feels eternal and ever-present within One's Being. A divine nakedness that feels so magical and right that it transcends all other moments in One's life. Nothing needs to be added or subtracted for it to be whole. One can often feel as if One is in direct contact with the Source point for all spiritual knowing and intuitive intelligence in the universe at the same time. This is where One realises the truth of One's existence. It is the moment where One is unbounded by One's humanity and exists in a pure state of divine consciousness. It can also be considered as the 'romantic bliss' that well-known writers and poets so eloquently allude to in One's creative works.

Feeling alone is not the same as being alone in the world. Often One can be in a crowded room of people and yet can feel very alone. However, One can be meditating in nature by oneself or at home and yet feel connected to everything in the universe in a state of oneness. Just because One is physically alone does not mean that One is personally lonely in life. One's egoic mind will often trick One into thinking that it needs to be kept busy to avoid that feeling of 'aloneness'. But it is only when One has stilled that thought within One's mind with silence that One can begin to feel a true sense of inner bliss, spiritual wholeness and divine contentment within oneself.

Even before One arrived on Earth and within One's mother's womb, One was not alone in the universe. One has always been connected to and spiritually entangled with other sentient Beings in this galaxy. The more One realises this fact, the more One will come to the presence of One's divine existence in the world and just how powerful a Being One is now.

Without realising it, One has the energy reserve and spiritual consciousness of the entire universe to draw on if need be. Similar to zero-point energy, One is able to access 'Source state existence' when One needs spiritual enhancement within One's life. Simply access it within One's deep meditative practices and align with Source consciousness to synergise with the light of existence itself. This is not a trick of the mind, it is a conscious entangled connection with the divine existence of the universe. To go within oneself is to know the oneness of One's inner Being. It is that simple – a sanctuary for One's spirit, soul or cosmic consciousness in this life.

The spiritual plane, realm or non-dimensional field of existence completely surrounds One, it penetrates One's existence, and it is part of the conscious fabric of the universe. All Beings exist in this ocean of existence. This is why One is not and can never be alone in the universe. Even if One's parents, family, friends or loved ones have moved on and returned to Source, the light of these Beings' existence is still present in the universe.

The universe wastes nothing as all things are repurposed in life. Even this solar system will eventually collapse in the future and return to star dust to be reborn into new planets and habitable worlds for life to begin the creative process again.

Take comfort in knowing that all relationships are impermanent. Everyone and every living thing will eventually die on Earth. This is not about being pessimistic, it is about being real and aware that One's mind–body is a functional part of the cycle of life. So, when One is alone then be alone and enjoy this time with oneself. The same is true when One is with another person, partner or parents. Celebrate life in the moments when One is in the company of others. Know the duality of living life when One is by oneself or when One is having a shared togetherness moment.

Take time out to be fully present in either situation. See life as a gift and One's aim should not be to rush through it but to stay completely awake along the journey as it unfolds. Ninety per cent of creating and experiencing wellness in One's life is simply showing up and being present at the moment as it is happening. Attract whatever One seeks through being it now and know that One will never be alone in this world.

The first seven years of life

The first seven years of a child's life are crucial to One's spiritual, mental and emotional development. During this time, a child's ego is emerging and One's personality and personhood are being established. Children during this time have a pure and genuine view of the world and are open to new experiences and insights. The sooner a child begins One's journey of realisation and awakening, the greater impact it will have on One's life trajectory.

Unfortunately, many modern cultures and societies disregard the importance of a child's spirit, soul, or cosmic consciousness and focus on egoic thoughts and self-identity. This is often due to a lack of exposure or understanding of spiritual concepts and fear-based agendas of the family, community, society, governing institutions and political structures.

However, there is a growing awakening on the planet, with people turning to spirituality and inner consciousness to bring about positive change. Raising consciousness in children during their first seven years of life is critical to this shift and creating a harmonious and spiritually aware society.

Every child on Earth is an expression of divine consciousness and a free spirit existing beyond space and time. Every person has the power to influence the world positively and what One believes, thinks, says, and does creates a ripple in the cosmic universe. One is important in the spiritual evolution of humanity and should never underestimate One's own power to bring about change.

This is why the first seven years of life on Earth are critical to the spiritual development of every person no matter what culture or society One was born into on the planet. During these critical years the emergence of One's ego takes place and the initial coding of One's personhood or living persona on Earth is established. At the same time, One will often see the spirit of a child with great clarity and without any social conditioning or ethnocultural filters. It is a beautiful experience to see how a child looks at the world with openness and wonder, discovering things for the first time.

During this time a child will say, do and observe things with little influence from One's ego and with a great divine insight into the world around One. There will be a purity to One's existence that is untarnished by ego. Children will express a genuineness and honesty that will pierce the very heart of the people around One with a love that is pure and directly connected to the Source of creation itself.

Often the process of realisation and awakening is seen as part of a later stage in the development of a person, but this is not true. The sooner the process of realisation and awakening takes place within a human, the greater effect it will have on the trajectory of a person's life in this world. Most parents on the planet waste great amounts of time on guiding, teaching and skilling children to attach to egoic thoughts of self-identity while giving no time or effort towards the realisation and recognition of the child's spiritual identity, sovereignty and existence in the universe.

The denial and disregard of a child's spirit, soul or cosmic consciousness is commonplace in many Western cultures and societies around the world. It is seen as hocus pocus and not critical to the overall wellness of a child or important to the wellbeing of an individual. This is due to the parents of this child being indoctrinated into not believing in One's own spirit, soul or cosmic consciousness or not having direct exposure to or experience of spirit. Most parents have been raised to ignore, invalidate and overlook anything to do with One's own spirit, soul or cosmic consciousness in the home, the family, at school or work and in society in general. There has been mass media suppression over many decades when it comes to acknowledging, accepting and adopting a spirit-centric point of view of the world. Most families, communities, societies and nation-states have adopted an ego-centric-based agenda and human living operating system which is principally fear-based.

One will not generally hear or be exposed to the discussion of spirit, soul or cosmic consciousness within modern society today because this threatens the existence of a person's own ego as well as established corrupt government institutions and political structures. The agenda of ego is to bring a dark or negative energy into the world that operates on attachments, judgements and resistance to change the way one thinks, lives, plays and works or is simply being in the world today.

However, this situation is changing with the ongoing awakening process on the planet. Many people are beginning to understand that news is not news anymore, it is entertainment. Important information is being diluted and swamped by fake and false truths or stories that pervert the light of awareness of One's own divine sovereignty and cosmic power. People are beginning to turn to the inner way of One's Being and others on the planet to harmonise with a new way of thinking, living, working, playing and being.

Raising the level of consciousness in the first seven years of life on the planet is important in bringing about a quantum shift in cosmic divine energy on Earth. It plays an important role in moving all people in the world to a new interstellar spiritually united Type 1 civilisation. This is the new path to personal prosperity and planetary abundance in the world.

The more people connect with other like-minded spiritually aware or awake people, the more this will support the growing tide of humanity to shift to a higher level of consciousness on the planet. Do not be disheartened or discouraged if this process is not happening fast enough for One. It is right on time and it is happening now. All One can do is awaken oneself completely and be a guiding light for others as everyone journeys along this personal path of self-realisation and inner awakening.

Know that One's divine light energy is infinitely greater than any ego-centric or negative energy in this world. What One believes, thinks, speaks and acts upon in life creates a cosmic ripple in the space–time continuum for all future generations. One is and has always been important in the spiritual evolution of humanity on Earth. Even though One may have not been taught, trained or tutored by a Master of spirituality in One's life, never underestimate the power One has to change oneself and thus influence the world in a positive direction.

What One does matters – today, tomorrow and forever.

Critical truths for every child on Earth

1. One is spirit, soul or cosmic consciousness (an eternal, immortal, and infinite spiritual Being of the universe)
2. One is a free spirit (existing beyond space and time [non-dimensional multi-state-based existence])
3. One is an expression of Source or divine consciousness (a sovereign spiritual entity or unique spiritual Being in an ocean of pure cosmic consciousness)
4. One exists in any or all seven states of divine consciousness (knowing, awareness, oneness, joy, free will, peace, and presence) at any given moment in the universe, plus an eighth state which is all states or whole of existence
5. One is host to One's human mind-body form (male, female, transgender or non-binary and manifested experiences in the universe)
6. One co-exists in a divine synergy of pure consciousness (spirit) and altered consciousness (mind-body)
7. One is here to awaken to One's spiritual reality, be present in this moment and manifest a new future on Earth now. This is all part of One's journey of infinite existence.

The false truth of One's ego

Being aware of and overcoming ego is an important step towards becoming a better version of oneself. By breaking free from the negative influence of ego, everyone can live a more fulfilling, meaningful and contented life, filled with love, freedom and positivity.

Ego is an important aspect of One's life that often goes unnoticed but shapes much of who One is and how One interacts with other people and the world around One. One's ego is essentially an ego-centric mindset that has been programmed into One's mind through various sources such as family, friends, society and the education system. Most people in the world are currently operating under this ego-centric mindset, largely unconscious of its influence on One's daily lives.

It is important to be aware of ego because it often leads to a life of control, judgement, power struggles, fear, scarcity and hate. This can lead to negative thoughts, attitudes, and behaviours that can negatively impact One's relationships and overall quality of life.

To understand and overcome ego, it is important to first recognise its existence within oneself. Knowing that ego is a part of everyone's lives and that all people have the power to change it is the first step towards freeing the whole world from its influence. By raising One's awareness of ego, One can better see and understand it, and rise above it to create a more prosperous, abundant and awakened life on Earth.

Most people currently living on Earth have uploaded a human living operating system into One's mind that is essentially ego-centric and not spirit-centric. This sociocultural conditioning and identity programming was accepted with One's full consent at the time. This living operating software has been continually reinforced and validated by One's family, friends, partners, society, community, First Nation and the nation-state in which One was raised. Various people, together with complicit educational institutions, taught, trained and tutored One's mind into believing in One's ego and deliberately disregarding, devaluing and dismissing anything that promotes, celebrates or aligns with One's spirit, soul or cosmic consciousness. This conditioned mental coding was first undertaken in the first seven years of life. This is when children spend most of One's time in alpha and theta brainwave cycles. During this time, most human children actively create foundation beliefs about oneself, relationships with others, life and the world that One lives in. A lot of these ideas and beliefs will remain unconscious throughout the rest of One's life and present as One's future behaviours, attitudes, achievements, future aspirational goals, how One chooses One's friends, life partners, direction in life and so on.

Between the ages of eight and twelve, One's additional mental programming will be further influenced. This is when One's core and primary thought processes will be shaped and neural pathways created with regard to the right way to think, behave, act and live a contemporary life. This period of time is directly related to the brainwave activity of a child's brain development and inner wiring. Amanda Gachot, a hypnotherapist, neuro-linguistic programming (NLP) and emotional freedom technique (EFT) practitioner, suggests and highlights correlations between ages of development in children and brainwave cycles.

What this means is that billions of people all around the world are currently unaware that One is living in a dream state or as an unawake person on the planet. Do not be surprised that One has been subjected to this process and is only now waking up to the truth of being influenced and shaped by this thought algorithm or social programming. While it may have taken decades to build the egoic coding and conditioning algorithms within One's mind, know that One can be free of this egoic framework and point of view in One's life. It is simply a matter of conscious awareness, choice and commitment.

> **The first step in avoiding the trap of ego is knowing of its existence.**

Age of development, brainwave cycles and stages of brain development

Age (years)	Brainwave (cycles per second)	Stages of brain development, internal coding and external programming
0-2	delta (0.5-4)	A newborn at this stage functions primarily from One's subconscious mind. Even in the womb, a baby is receiving its external programming in this state. To aid in its survival outside the womb, a newborn baby knows how to copy or mimic One's features when One smiles or gestures, which is crucial in building rapport and emotional attachment to One's caregiver. Adults in deep sleep are also in delta.
2-6	theta (4-8)	At this stage, children are very connected to One's internal world. Imagination, daydreaming and make-believe are important operating spaces for the mind. Critical, rational and logical thinking is not present yet. In this 'super learning' state, every child is very open to suggestions. This is the period when the programming layers of 'truth and belief' are accepted and neural connections are formed in a child's brain. People who undergo hypnosis therapy and animals operate in this frequency.
5-8	alpha (8-13)	The analytical mind begins to form at this stage. The environment is a source of information from which children interpret and draw conclusions. Children operate in both the inner world of imagination and outer world of 'perceived reality'. Know that when One meditates or in a peaceful relaxed trance, One's brain is in alignment with the same frequency. This is the perfect state to create new ideas, brain storm in a group, manifest powerful life-changing moments or learn new things.
8-12+	beta (13+)	This is when most conscious and analytical thinking occurs in human beings. The mind is focused, alert and capable of logical thinking (left hemisphere of the brain). Adults spend most of One's time in this cycle.

Through raising One's awareness of ego within oneself and others, One is better able to see it, know it and rise above it. When One can see through the veil of ego, One is on the right path to know oneself completely.

Being aligned to ego (in One's mind) is about expressing the human vibration of control, judgement, power, separation, fear, scarcity and hate. However, being in alignment with spirit (centred within One's heart or heart chakra) is about expressing the vibration of openness, flow and freedom, non-judgement, shared responsibility, unity, love and peace, abundance and acceptance, and non-resistance to change.

To be a person with an ego-centric mind is to live a life that is principally fear-based. To be a person with a spirit-centric mind is to live from a love-based perspective, knowing that the universe is always on One's side and that everything will work out in the end.

As One begins to understand and come to terms with this duality of expressed human existence, One will be able to observe whatever is in One's mind without attachment, judgement or resistance. The best way to lift the fog of ego in One's mind is through inner self-realisation and mindful meditative practices on a daily basis.

> **Whatever thought One has had in the past does not determine One's present future now.**

Know that nothing is fixed in this world. One's reality is being continually reshaped, recreated and reconfigured from moment to moment. This means that One can change the trajectory of One's life simply by shifting the vibrations of One's thoughts from ego-centric to spirit-centric. One does this by becoming self-aware and looking inwards toward One's spirit, soul or cosmic consciousness. The universe invites One to shine as brightly as One can in this world. It is important that One believes in the truth of One's higher self and the sentient presence One has in the world today.

To connect with others from a place of ego is to operate at a lower vibration or negative dark energy, but being aligned to spirit is operating at a high vibration and increased level of consciousness as well as positive energy in this world. Ego does what it has always done to contain, control and capture people's imagination, lifestyles and living experiences through a belief in fear and limitations. Spirit is always about being free and embracing the unknown as well as expanding One's consciousness and creative intelligence into the universe.

One must make a choice. Does One choose to live, be and create a life in a world build on previous intergenerational deterministic and conditioned egoic beliefs, thoughts, behaviours, habits and practices? Or, does One choose to be true to One's higher self and live a life where One values and practices align with One's spirit, soul or cosmic consciousness? A life where One is free and expanding One's consciousness into the galaxy and universe, where One is able to manifest a new reality on Earth that is committed to consciously co-creating an interstellar spiritually united Type 1 civilisation.

If One's heart is drawn to the second reality on Earth, One will feel it within One's inner Being. Do not be afraid to journey along this path in life. Just do it. Let One's inner spirit and the universe guide One along 'the way'. Ego will have a million reasons why something cannot or never be done or achieved. Spirit only requires one single belief in a new vision or reality plus the commitment to manifest and attract it into One's life now. The false truth of ego will always over-promise and under-deliver, but spirit makes no such promises and requires only a belief in One's higher self to manifest the changes that One seeks in this world. To believe in spirit, soul or cosmic consciousness is to know the divinity within oneself and all interstellar sentient Beings in the universe.

Being a spiritual entity in the universe

Being spiritual or recognising One's inner spirit is crucial in today's world for personal growth, inner development and human evolution. External validation and pleasure from material things will always be fleeting and temporary, while the internal joy of being connected to One's spirit is permanent. The seven key virtues – compassion, helpfulness, acceptance, generosity, simplicity, patience and openness – offer a pathway to connecting with One's spirit and the universe. It is important for individuals to question One's own beliefs and become aware of One's own spiritual sovereignty and divinity, rather than relying on external saviours.

The pursuit of fame and fortune is an illusion created to distract individuals from the real purpose of awakening to One's inner spirit. There are various groups on the planet with negative intentions who aim to control and manipulate the population, but these people's efforts will ultimately fail due to the unstoppable awakening process and convergence of timelines towards an interstellar spiritually united Type 1 civilisation on Earth.

Every living Being on Earth has the divine power to bring positivity and awareness to the world, and more and more people are awakening to One's spirit every day. It is important to recognise the connection to all life on the planet and to bring light and wellness to the conversation to create a positive future for all.

The choice is simple: to believe in One's spirit, soul or cosmic consciousness or not. It is time to stop chasing external validation or gratification from someone else with regard to One's inner spirit. It is important to know that what lies within oneself is far greater than anything that can be obtained or attained in the outside world. Eventually, One will come to realise that the happiness of all external pleasures is like water flowing through One's fingers. One will never be able to hold on to it, only experience it in the moment when it is present.

However, as a spirit, One's internal joy is forever imbued within One's Being. One need only align with it by being generous with all that One is and has to offer in this life.

Virtues offer One a gateway to One's spirit and the universe. For each of the seven key virtues, there is a corresponding state of spiritual consciousness.

Key virtues and key states of consciousness

Key virtues	Key states of consciousness
Compassion	Knowing
Helpfulness	Awareness
Acceptance	Oneness
Generosity	Joy
Simplicity	Free will
Patience	Peace
Openness	Presence

The only question that One must ask oneself is: To be ... spirit or not to be ... spirit? This is the only real and valid question One must consider if One is going to evolve on this planet. Is One going to hide behind the veil of ego in One's mind or is One going to rise to the challenge and become all that One is meant to be in this world? Never mind what countless generations of people have done or believed in before One arrived on Earth. One must think for oneself, believe for oneself and act in One's own spiritual best interest. Do not rely upon an external saviour, mystical person, shaman, 'God', 'Allah' or Great Creator Being coming to Earth to save One, anybody or the planet from danger or difficulty. One needs to face the reality that if a super Being did exist in the universe, it would have already done so.

Hence, One is here to awaken to One's own spiritual sovereignty and cosmic divinity. This will enable One to move along a path of enlightenment and continue One's eternal journey across the universe. This is why it is crucial that One finds an inner way for oneself in this world. Be aware that it is highly likely that interstellar intelligence and cosmic Beings of advanced consciousness are already in contact with people on Earth.

> *To be empowered – to be free, to be unlimited, to be creative, to be genius, to be divine – that is who you are ... Once you feel this way, memorise this feeling; remember this feeling. This is who you really are.*
> Dr Joe Dispenza

The pursuit of personal social fame and individual global fortune in this world is an illusion created by ego-centric people to keep the population of the planet distracted from the real and only worthwhile activity. The activity that so many ego-centric people in appointed and elected positions of power are concerned with is the 'awakening process' happening here on Earth now. Covert groups operating in secret within established governance structures are held together by negative energy forces. The agenda of these groups is to corrupt the timeline so that human consciousness will not vibrate at a higher level and people will remain silent in One's ignorance and become complicit to being mindlessly brainwashed and programmed into accepting a false narrative of the future.

The good news is that these people and this agenda to poison, pervert and prevent the 'awakening process' will fail. It will fail for two reasons. The first is that One is unable to stop the 'awakening process' on Earth once it has already begun. The second is due to the convergence of timelines to a point of singularity. Beyond this point, only one possible event horizon will exist. The event horizon beyond this singularity will align with the universe. What will arise is a united spiritually based Type 1 civilisation on Earth.

As part of this process, two divergent cultures of people will emerge on Earth. One rogue group of people with nefarious intentions will aim to control who, how, when, where and why certain things are to be done, undertaken and managed across various populations on the planet. This group sees the future as an opportunity to maintain personal power over other people in the hope that it will be able to ensure its survival and privilege. It will use the existing political and non-political global corporate processes to manipulate information and suppress freedom of thought and speech across the world. This action will be undertaken through invasive digital strategies and targeted viral algorithms, which already exist today on social media platforms.

One is grateful that within every living sentient Being on Earth there exists a divine creative energy that can transmute, transform and transcend any and all dark negative energies in this world. One has the indomitable power to bring a spiritual light of awareness and divine wellness to the conversation to change the trajectory and create a positive outcome for everyone living on Earth today. The lives of everyone matter and One is connected to all life on the planet.

With each passing day, more and more people will begin to awaken to One's spirit, soul or cosmic consciousness. The population of the entire planet will eventually reach a tipping point of conscious change. This change will be to align to a common, shared or singular consciousness. As the future unfolds it will become more and more obvious which people have core ego-centric programming or agendas. The motives of these people will manifest through a projection of individual personal power, separation, greed, hate, control and economic enslavement of other people. The more this rogue group of people try and hold on to power, the more it will escape One's grip. It will be like trying to catch One's shadow or hold air in One's hand.

The benefit of choosing to be a spiritual sentient Being is that One will be joining with billions of other Beings in creating a new future on Earth. A future that is focused on co-creating an interstellar spiritually based Type 1 civilisation that will enable prosperity, abundance and an awakened living, working, playing and being for all in this world. When One believes in One's spirit, soul or cosmic consciousness, One creates a way to manifest a new reality now. Being spirit is a gateway to the secrets of the universe and One's awakened presence.

Flowing with freedom along One's spiritual path

Flowing with freedom along one's spiritual path is essential to unlocking the infinite potential to change One's life and future now. Embrace One's inner awareness and allow oneself to flow with life, breaking free from the limitations imposed by family, community, society and cultural programming.

'Going with the flow' along One's spiritual path is essential to finding true inner peace, joy and contentment in life. It is important to recognise that One is already a free spirit in the universe, but may have been taught to limit oneself with social conditioning and cultural programming. However, through self-realisation, observation and meditation, One can free the mind and uncover One's true spiritual identity. It is crucial to understand that One is not defined by One's thoughts, beliefs, past experiences, or actions, but is instead an infinite and eternal spiritual Being.

It is also important to acknowledge One's divine responsibility to One's spiritual sovereignty and cosmic destiny. This involves breaking free from the mass global indoctrination to simply be human and embracing One's inner awareness of One's spirit, soul, or cosmic consciousness. The path to inner freedom does not lie outside of oneself, but instead exists within.

To live a life of freedom, it is essential to be present in the moment and aware of all that is happening around oneself. If One finds oneself on autopilot, going through life aimlessly, it is time to pause and reflect on One's situation. Life should not just be a series of duties, responsibilities and obligations. Instead, it is about being free in mind, body and spirit.

To truly feel free, one must let go of pain and suffering, remove all attachments and judgements, and simply flow with the universe. The key to living freely is to think, act, and live freely, enabling a sense of freedom in all aspects of life. The ultimate goal is to align with the universe and become a beacon of freedom for others.

Freedom is something that One must give oneself in this world. It cannot be given to save another person, it can only be truly claimed for oneself in life. As a free spirit, One has the ability to go and be anywhere in the universe. From an early age, One may have been taught to choose to imprison One's mind and life with One's own egoic social conditioning and cultural programming. This process would have most likely taken decades to learn, but it can be unlearned by observing One's thoughts and thought processes. In addition, meditative and mindful practices can greatly assist oneself to free the mind and reveal the truth of who One really is in this world.

For everything that One's mind thinks about oneself – One is not. For everything that One believes oneself to be today – One is not. One is not One's past or whatever One has achieved in life. One is not One's mistakes or misadventures. One is not anything that One has done or undone, configured or reconfigured, moved or removed. One as a spiritual Being is not attached to anything that One has been part of or a participant in this life. One is free of all obligations to others, as these individuals also move along One's own path of self-realisation and inner awakening.

However, One does have an incredibly important divine responsibility to One's spiritual sovereignty and cosmic destiny in life. Very few people will speak of this special duty to being One's true and authentic spiritual self, as it challenges most people's existing human identities and belief systems in the world today. It goes against the mass global indoctrination to 'only be human'. Most people on the planet today have been mindlessly programmed over decades to not think for oneself, to not believe in oneself and to not feel that One is worthy of greatness within. People, families, communities and societies have purposely, intentionally and collectively suppressed this inner awareness of One's spirit, soul or cosmic consciousness. This is why there is a great void and sense of lacking in people's lives all across the world, which people try to fill up with external things like accumulating unnecessary material objects, ongoing personal relationships and new stimulating experiences. The answer to inner freedom in life does not lie outside oneself, it exists within One now. It always has and always will. The inner way is within oneself – this is the solution that has always existed as part of One's divine Being.

To create freedom in One's life, One must first acknowledge the abundance of it in the universe. If One's mind–body is on autopilot and simply going aimlessly through life from one appointment to another, One needs to pause, stop what One is currently doing and deeply reflect on this situation. Life is not meant to be an endless stream of personal or parental duties, work tasks or job priorities and social responsibilities or cultural obligations.

Life is so much more than this. Living free is very much about being where One is now. It does not matter where One is on the planet. Being present at the moment and being awake to all that is – this is key to being free.

Learn to recognise the signs when One's egoic mind is driving One to get things done or constantly staying busy. If things are forced or generally uncomfortable, this is usually an important sign that One is letting One's ego into the driver's seat of One's life. It is time to change the way One is living life. One will need to consciously improve or upgrade One's core human operating system to an intentional place of spiritual awareness.

Know that One was born free and will die free. One has always been a free spirit unbounded by time or space in the universe. One has just been so caught up in the mental matrix of this world that One has lost sight of this state of existence. But One can change One's life and lifestyle today. Simply begin where One is now. Aim to be an expression of freedom by aligning in perfect harmony, balance and synchronicity with the universe itself.

To be free is to feel free within One's mind–body–spirit. This feeling of being free is in part a recognition of the abundance of freedom in the universe and bringing this waking living experience into One's life at this moment. Imagine it – believe it – co-create it now as part of One's reality. When One creates space in One's life, One is facilitating new opportunities to think freely, act freely, speak freely, live freely and simply just be free.

Living free is about enabling a sense of freedom in everything One thinks, says, actions and is now. This means letting go of pain and suffering by removing all attachments, judgements and resistance to change and simply flowing with 'the way' of the universe.

Suffering is due entirely to clinging or resisting. It is a sign of our unwillingness to move on, to flow with life.
Sri Nisargadatta Maharaj

One can rise above the pain and suffering by truly knowing that One is spirit, soul or cosmic consciousness. An eternal infinite sentient Being of the universe – today, tomorrow – for eternity. Be aware that One has the infinite potential to change One's life and future at this present moment. As One changes in each and every moment, One becomes a brighter beacon of freedom for oneself and others living on the planet.

To experience freedom in every waking living moment of One's life, realise that One is imbued with conscious 'free will' to change anything and everything within One now. As a beautiful Being of light, love and oneness, One is pure divine consciousness from Source.

Awakening One's own spiritual sovereignty along 'the way' also enables One's freedom in this life. One will become more interested in being all that One can be than trying to fit into an egoic world.

As One begins to flow with freedom in every aspect of One's life, One will begin to experience amazing synchronicities and moments of serendipity. This all correlates to realising who One truly is and being 'awake' now.

Being an inspiration in the world

To inspire others, One must first inspire oneself in this life. If One has a calling to be an inspiration in this world, make an effort to seek out, study and connect with amazing people from the past and in the present who are great beacons of light, hope and inspiration. The ability to inspire others can be seen as an art, but it is much more than this. Inspiration is an important leadership skill that separates great leaders from ordinary ones.

Most people who have achieved greatness in One's life have done so through personal suffering, individual sacrifice and social separation in pursuit of One's vision, mission and commitment to oneself, others and a new future. A good leader is able to create a fusion of belief, passion and energy coupled with dedication through One's mindful actions, attitudes, behaviours, habits and practices.

One will often find those awesome leaders show a high level of honesty, genuineness and integrity. Great inspirational leaders do not fear time. These leaders see all failures as a learning opportunity to improve and become better in One's life. A good leader will be able to share and clearly explain One's vision for the future, why One is travelling along this path, who will benefit, how it will improve the world and how One intends to get there.

Inspirational leaders operate at a high vibrational energy level and have an inclusive, open and collaborative approach to life. These types of people begin with the vision in mind but are open to the best way forward in manifesting this new reality now. There is no 'right' or 'wrong' idea, suggestion or way to achieve the desired outcome. The most important tool that One uses is to 'think outside of the box' by imagining creative solutions, using unconditional positivity together with an optimistic outlook for the future.

Good spiritual leaders, like all other inspirational leaders, lead by showing and sharing One's divine knowledge and eternal wisdom. These people do not instruct others about individual inspiration. One simply nurtures and nourishes the spirit, soul or cosmic consciousness with the truth of who One is as well as how to extinguish pain and suffering from One's life.

> Inspirational people simply think, speak and act intentionally to be One's true and authentic self. This is the key that enables other people to ignite One's own spark of inspiration to co-create a better world and future for all.

To inspire oneself and others in life can often create a great unforeseen outcome. This is where One's potential energy and applied action results in a higher level of engagement and commitment in whatever One is involved in at the time. It can also ignite a new spark of inspiration within oneself.

> **Believe unconditionally in One's ability to inspire oneself and others to change, transform and act intentionally to benefit all. This is 'the way' to co-create a new reality, new future and new Earth.**

Various traits or characteristics are ascribed to people with truly inspirational leadership styles. An inspirational leader will:
- commit to values and virtues
- invest in personal and professional development
- be genuine and authentic
- be skilled in communicating and negotiating with others
- promote a shared unity and work–life journey
- be approachable, open and inclusive
- accept vulnerability and risk.

Commit to values and virtues

Inspirational leaders have a deep sense of responsibility to others and act in One's best interests. These types of people are driven by One's values and virtues to create positive change within oneself, with others and in the world. Most leaders possess a good understanding of One's values and virtues and know how to pivot in order to engage effectively with others to facilitate a good outcome. Even when the pressure of the situation increases, One does not crumble to popular demands or take the easy way out because One's decisions and directions may cause discomfort to people with egoic minds and attitudes.

Inspirational leaders operate with a moral and ethical compass in One's life and instil trust in others because One acts with genuine care and a high level of personal integrity. One's daily practice is about staying true to One's spirit and principles, which are imbued in everything that One says, does and actions. A good leader is disciplined, determined and dedicated to fulfilling One's vision each and every day. One makes a daily effort to stay on track but will quickly adjust One's path or make a course correction if need be.

Invest in personal and professional development

Leaders are committed to continual quality improvement in oneself. One understands the importance of investing in One's ongoing personal and professional development. One is not shy about making mistakes, taking responsibility for One's actions, attitudes or comments and improving One's practice. One realises that if One gets the inside right, the outside will take care of itself. Inspirational leaders project a confident sense of self as well as being aware of One's personal limitations, skills and abilities. One realises that One does not know everything and will seek out others to assist, help and mentor One along 'the way' in life. One is aware that change is not without pain and growth. So, One is willing to step into the unknown in order to co-create a better version of oneself. As One moves forward in life, One uses every living experience – 'good' or 'bad' – to transform oneself and reconfigure One's life to align with One's higher self and vision of a new reality.

Be genuine and authentic

Being a genuinely authentic leader is recognised by many as a distinguished and important quality. People in businesses, communities and modern society highly value this trait or characteristic in leaders. Leaders know One's personal story and what it took for One to be where One is today. Many are willing to share this journey of hardship, hope and happiness with others in order to create a shared togetherness and common ground. One is proud of where One has come from, the challenges One has overcome and the special qualities which makes One unique.

A leader will often talk about the courage needed to meet a challenge and be successful in life. One is not afraid to stand up for the truth or confront social injustice in the world. One will call out or draw attention to ego-centric *Acts*, policies or practices in order to highlight where change needs to happen. One treats all with care, kindness and compassion as well as dignity and respect. One is true to oneself and others no matter the situation, circumstance or social event.

Be skilled in communicating and negotiating with others

There are various verbal and non-verbal (i.e. body language) communication styles that inspirational leaders are good at and use when engaging with people, partners and at professional workplaces. A good leader can assess people's social mannerisms, emotional intelligence or personal behavioural cues and adapt One's communication style to match, mirror or suit the audience. One knows that chatting with a family member or someone in business or anybody in the community requires slightly different approaches and styles. The art of communication is a highly valued skill, as is the ability to negotiate places, processes and paths in life. One is able to see the simplicity in complex situations and communicate it in a way that is user-friendly, easy to understand and reaches people.

One is patient and allows space for others to participate in the conversation without expectation. One is mindful of what One says and how it may impact others. One chooses One's words carefully and always responds in a positive way when replying or giving constructive positive feedback. One is very mindful of focusing on the issue, concern or worry and not the person when seeking suggestions or communicating creative solutions in the world.

Promote a shared unity and work-life flow

An inspirational leader understands that to achieve anything in this world requires the cooperation of other sentient Beings. Collaboration and working in partnership are essential for achieving any and all desired outcomes in life. Lateral trust between people is critical in creating a mutual win-win environment for motivating and manifesting success in people's lives. One does this by enabling an innovative culture that is all about improving, growing and learning in a supportive way. This is key to promoting goodwill and a common vision for the future. When One is not focused on One's own ego it allows individuals to come together in a safe space to share One's experiences, knowledge, opinion and ideas.

Great achievements and results are often realised by people when One has let go of the outcome and simply focuses on doing one simple thing with great attention to detail, love or passion and devotion. It is important for a leader to set the pace of progress and flow with the natural rhythm, harmony and synchronicity of the universe.

Be approachable, open and inclusive

Inspirational leaders build and create a sense of belonging and safe space for people. Individuals then feel confident in approaching and discussing key issues, concerns or worries, knowing that One is able to freely talk without judgement or being viewed harshly for doing so. Good leaders see diversity as a strength, not a weakness. One is able to demonstrate a sense of comfortableness within One's own skin. One works to cultivate a culture of openness, acceptance and inclusiveness at home, in the community and in the workplace. One accepts everything and rejects nothing as One's starting point in life. As part of One's personal and professional practice, One has chosen to adopt a mindful outlook that welcomes the unique differences of others and alternative perspectives. When people feel psychologically safe, One is inclined to trust others and take acceptable risks in improving performance and working towards achieving the outcome.

Inspirational leaders treat others fairly and with respect but are also firm on important messaging about valuing the partnership or relationship, acknowledging the contributions of others and working proactively in a spirit of mutual cooperation that benefits all. This approach is not fear-based. It is all about promoting, motivating and bringing out the best in people through One's individual passion and collective capacity to be open, honest and real with people.

Accept vulnerability and risk

An inspirational leader is not afraid to trust oneself and take courageous risks in life without the certainty of a successful outcome. It is only when One is willing to step into the unknown with all of One's mind–body–spirit and risk great failure that One will receive a great reward. This type of person sees opportunities not obstacles, an adventure not adversity and a journey of exploration not a justification for an excuse. Being vulnerable is not thinking lesser of oneself, it is simply being open to the possibility of an opportunity that may change or even physically or emotionally impact oneself in a positive or negative way.

A good leader will own One's mistakes and turn these experiences into learning moments to improve or co-create oneself into a better person. One radiates a deep sense of passion and optimism for oneself, life and the universe. One also has a willingness and determination to apply oneself (mind–body–spirit) to co-create a new reality, new vision and new world. The motto "Who Dares Wins' is attributed to the British SAS. It reminds One that only intentional effort creates intentional results or outcomes in life. Inspirational leaders know this and embody a solution-focused approach together with ongoing adaptation to manifest One's future vision, no matter the challenges before One or along 'the way'.

IMPORTANT LEARNINGS, TEACHINGS AND POINTINGS

Key ways to being a sentient Being of the universe

01 Realise that as spirit, soul or cosmic consciousness, One is not alone in the universe – One never has been and never will be. One is spiritually entangled with all other sentient Beings in an ocean of pure cosmic consciousness or a unified field of infinite possibilities.

02 Clearly understand the distinction between the false truth of One's ego and the truth of One's spirit, soul or cosmic consciousness. Know that the daily practising of One's key virtues is a gateway to One's inner states of consciousness such as knowing, awareness, oneness, joy, free will, peace and presence (there is also an eighth state, which is all states in unity or a whole-of-consciousness state of existence).

03 When One freely and intentionally chooses to be spirit, soul or cosmic consciousness, One is creating an inner coherence of mind–body–spirit. This enables new living experiences and a spirit-centric lifestyle that is in alignment with the natural rhythm, harmony and synchronicity of the universe. As One journeys along 'the way' of the awakening process, One is co-creating and manifesting a new future, new reality and new Earth now.

 One is here to awaken to One's own spiritual sovereignty and cosmic divinity.

 To experience freedom in every waking living moment of One's life, realise that One is imbued with conscious 'free will' to change anything and everything within One now. As a beautiful Being of light, love and oneness, One is pure divine consciousness from Source.

 Believe unconditionally in One's ability to inspire oneself and others to change, transform and act intentionally to benefit all. This is 'the way' to co-create a new reality, new future and new Earth today.

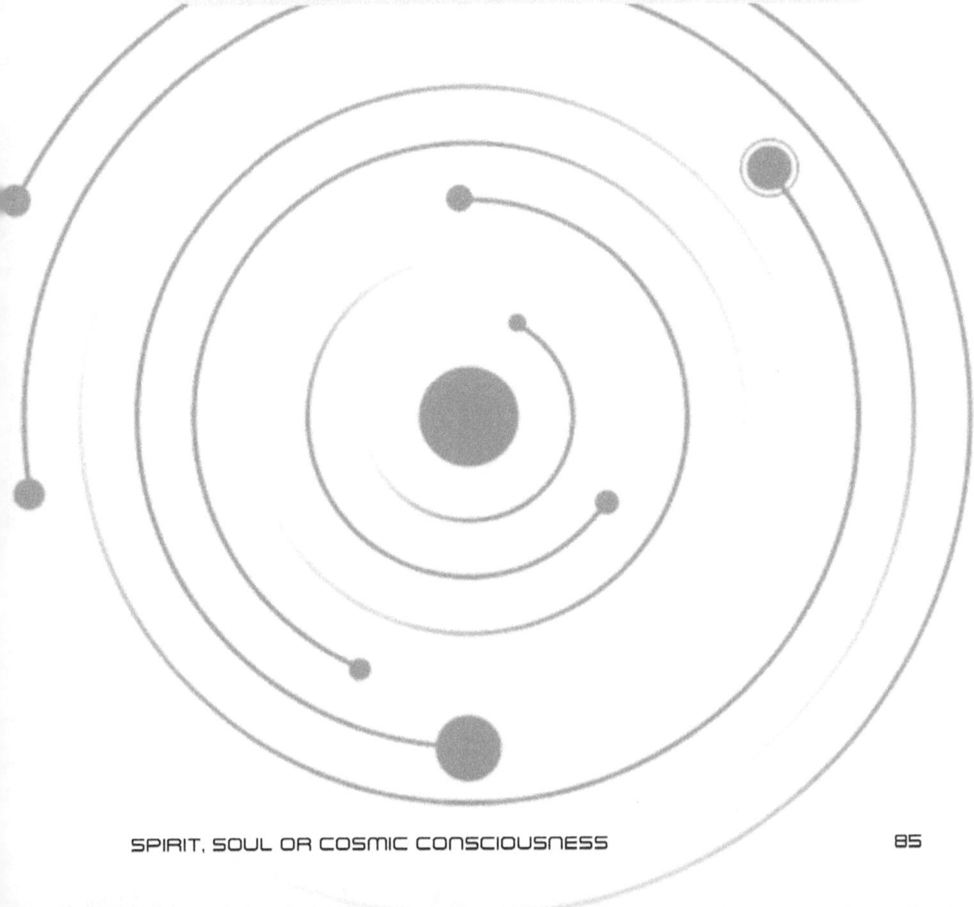

PART THREE

Transmute One's spiritual existence

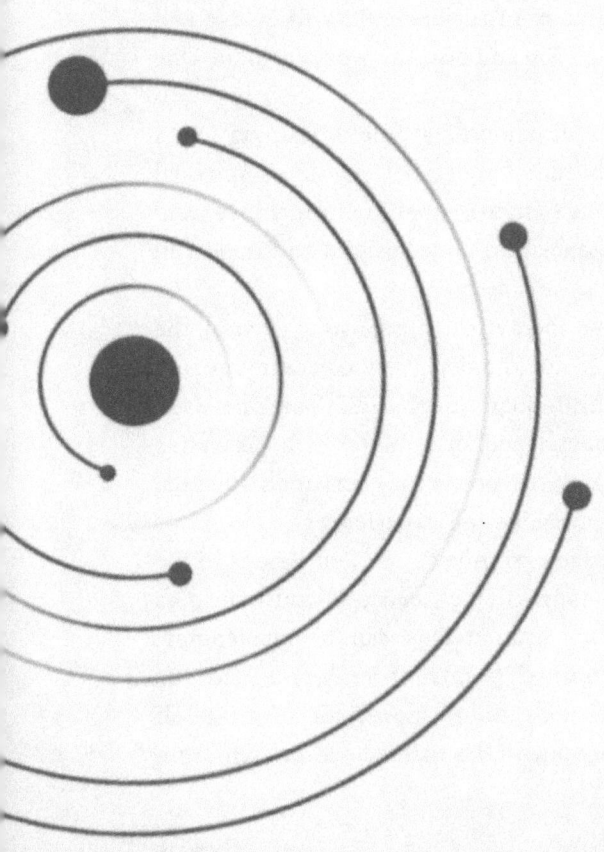

One's spiritual presence on Earth

By embracing One's spiritual presence, One takes on the responsibility of One's thoughts, feelings and actions, and becomes an incredibly powerful interdimensional force in the universe. The manifestation of a new reality begins with a spiritual awareness of who One truly is and the infinite potential One possesses. By embracing One's spiritual presence on Earth, One has the opportunity to evolve and transform both One's individual life and also the world around One as well.

Spiritual presence on Earth plays a crucial role in shaping One's life and the world One lives in today. By embracing One's spiritual identity, One can tap into One's divine inner light and love, and transform One's spiritual existence into a meaningful and impactful presence on Earth.

Max Planck was a German theoretical physicist who won the Nobel Prize in Physics in 1918 for the discovery of energy quanta and is considered the originator of quantum physics. Planck believed that consciousness is fundamental and that matter is a derivative of consciousness. This highlights the power of everyone's spiritual consciousness in shaping One's reality and experiences.

It is important to acknowledge everyone as sentient Beings in the universe with the capacity to express One's spiritual consciousness through One's human form or avatar. This can be challenging, especially if One has only limited points of reference and life experiences, but it all starts with a genuine appreciation for oneself at this moment. It may also require One to distance oneself from negative energy and people who may react unkindly to One's spiritual beliefs.

The state of inner presence, as part of the seven pure states of consciousness, is achieved through the practice of openness. Being open to everything and attached to nothing allows oneself to connect with others and see the world with clarity, free from self-imposed limitations. As One becomes more present in One's life, One will experience a range of positive changes, including synchronicities, effortless connections, and an intentional influence over One's life and destiny on Earth and in this solar system.

As a sentient Being of the universe, One has the capacity to transmute One's spiritual existence into an amazing living presence on Earth today. Know this core truth and give oneself permission to express One's divine inner light, love and oneness. Now is the right time and Earth is the right place for One to embrace One's authentic spiritual identity and affirm One's spiritual sovereignty.

One also has the infinite potential to manifest a new reality on Country (land, sea and sky), in the world and universe. One simply needs to begin from a place of spiritual awareness and know who One truly is in the universe. The manifestation of any material form or experience is in direct proportion to One's state and expression of spiritual consciousness within and through One's human form.

One might ask oneself this question: How does One create a spiritual presence on Earth when One has limited points of reference and life experiences? The answer is to begin by acknowledging oneself as a sentient Being of the universe. One does this by being open, honest and having a genuine sense of loving appreciation for oneself in this world at this moment in time. Say to oneself: 'One has always been and will always be – spirit, soul or cosmic consciousness'. Realise that this inner truth is undeniable and an inescapable part of One's divine identity and spiritual sovereignty in the universe.

There are many people on the planet who may react in an unkind way to this thought and suggestion. Some may scoff or try to belittle this statement of belief about One's spirit. These people are often operating from an ego-centric mind or negative mental framework in an effort to shame, embarrass or humiliate One's intentions to align with One's higher self. A person who does this typically wants others to not vibrate at a high level of conscious existence on the planet. There is nothing that One can say or do to convince these people to open One's mind to an alternative way of living, working and being on Earth. The best that One can hope for is that these individuals self-realise One's own inner spiritual truth. While this is happening, it is important that One creates distance from this destructive and damaging energy so One can focus on forming new connections with other like-minded spiritually aware and awake people on the planet.

As hard as it may seem, One may need to let go of people with negative vibrational energy so One is not constantly living in a toxic and contaminated work-life-social environment. One will need to take intentional action to upgrade One's friendship circle, life partner, business associates or living cultural networks. Taking this kind of action may not be easy at first but it will be worth it in the end.

Know that this all takes time, space and an intentional effort to make positive changes in One's life. The best place to begin is to start right now. Just start here in this moment today. Know that when One is aligned to One's inner spirit – all the answers will come to One, just be patient.

Everything is flowing within the universe and One is part of this infinite river of cosmic synchronicity.

Presence is one of the seven pure states of consciousness within every sentient Being in the universe. Practicing the virtue of 'openness' is a gateway to the state of inner presence within One's Being. By being open to everything and attached to nothing within One's mind, One is allowing everyone and everything to simply be present as it is, unfiltered by One's sociocultural programming or past events.

When One is open, One is able to see more clearly and can spiritually connect with others in the same space. One's mind will be free from the constraints of self-talk that suggests things need to be a certain way for One to be fully present in this space. As One becomes more and more present in life, One's mind–body–spirit will align in a state of coherence within the unified field of infinite possibilities. In this state of coherence, One will notice a range of things begin to automatically happen, as if guided by an all-powerful magical divine force.

Synchronicities will start to occur in One's life. People will show up in One's life as if they were meant to be there all along. Connections will happen with a sense of effortlessness and things will simply flow like water along a river towards an aligned outcome. One will begin to operate from a space of 'intentionality' in the moment. One will begin to recognise One's inner spiritual presence as a very real interdimensional force in the universe. One will realise that One has the infinite capacity to intentionally influence One's life in any way or direction that One perceives it flowing in. One does this by simply bringing One's vision or imagined destiny into the now of One's living presence on Earth.

When One is truly intentionally present in One's life, One is taking extreme responsibility as a spiritual Being for One's beliefs, thoughts and actions in this world. Whatever is happening, One fully accepts custodianship of One's current thoughts, feelings, attitudes, behaviours, habits and expressed communication (verbal and non-verbal) in One's wellships, partnerships or relationships. One does not assign any blame to another individual for One's lack of something or limiting beliefs in One's life. One does not use any excuses, such as One's parents did not love One, One did not go to college or university, One was born in a developing country, One was raised in poverty, One has no friends or family, or One did not have any good teachers, mentors or support networks. One can view all of these social, cultural and economic settings as simply an opportunity to be the best that One can be in life and on this planet.

Everything that exists in your life does so because of two reasons: something you did or something that you didn't do.
Albert Einstein

This universe is what One makes and creates within it. If One believes it is a cruel, harsh and unforgiving place – so be it. But if One believes it is a benevolent, kind and giving place – so be it. Whatever One chooses to believe, One will be right.

One is powerful beyond measure and One's presence in this world does make a difference. One simply needs to figure out how One will go about creating change in One's own life so that it positively influences all that is around One now. Never underestimate One's spiritual presence to shape the future of humanity and create an interstellar spiritually united Type 1 civilisation on Earth now. One's presence has the power to shape and reconfigure One's life into something truly amazing, beautiful and wonderful today.

Expressing One's infinite existence

Expressing One's infinite spiritual existence is a powerful tool for personal growth and spiritual evolution. It holds the potential to bring about a harmonious, spiritually united and awakened world. By embracing this truth, One has the power to shape the fabric of space–time and manifest a new future reality on Earth today.

It involves embracing the truth that one is not just a physical being, but a spiritual Being existing in this world and universe. Accepting this truth allows One access to alternative dimensions and to travel beyond One's current 3D construct into other spiritual planes or realms.

To enable this requires a paradigm shift to a higher level of consciousness within One's Being. This shift is facilitated through daily practices such as meditation, breath work, and aligning One's mind, body and spirit to resonate with an inner coherence. It is important to note that this process does not require supervision, external validation or approval from others.

Once fully realised, expressing One's infinite existence leads to profound changes in One's life. It goes so far as altering the current trajectory and reconfiguring One's destiny on Earth and in this solar system. One begins to see the ongoing futility of both active and passive egoic systems and structures that promote the oppression of humanity on this planet. This realisation is a crucial step towards spiritual empowerment and a shift towards a more harmonious world.

Moreover, expressing One's infinite existence is also a reminder that human death is an illusion. It is only a spiritual doorway back to Source and One's pure consciousness in the universe. One's spirit, soul, or cosmic consciousness continues to exist beyond the concepts of time and space, and is unable to 'traditionally die'.

To change the world and universe, One must first begin by giving oneself permission to change the belief that One has about oneself. After all, One's mind–body–spirit is a work in progress and not a fixed point in space–time. This all begins with a paradigm shift to a higher level of conscious existence within One's Being. It is all about realising that One is spirit, soul or cosmic consciousness now. To rephrase it another way: *One exists – so One is.*

There has never been a more important time in One's life to change how One perceives and recognises oneself in this world and universe. Only the person reading this text can create One's access to higher dimensions of existence in this life.

The time is now to awaken to the truth of One's infinite existence in the universe. When One fully embraces and accepts this fundamental truth, an interdimensional portal of spiritual awareness will be opened. This portal of spiritual awareness will give One access to the wisdom of the universe, interstellar Beings and other known galaxies.

Once One has opened this gateway within One's Being, One will have accessed an inner awareness and awakened to this existing spiritual truth and universal wisdom. One will never be able to live life in an unawakened way or in a dream state on the planet ever again.

This change will be so profound it will literally alter the trajectory of One's life on Earth. In doing so, One's living destiny will be reconfigured and reorganised by One's spiritual intent more than One's past ego-centric programming or current social conditioning. One will realise that One is powerful beyond measure and able to shape the very fabric of space–time or the unified field of infinite possibilities in which One exists now. One will recognise that what others perceive as reality is only a vibrating material construct or altered consciousness which is able to be manifested into anything that One can imagine.

The more One believes in oneself as spirit, soul or cosmic consciousness, the more the universe will support and align with the coherence of One's mind–body–spirit in everyday life.

> **With a great belief comes a great awakening to the truth of One's existence.**

As One begins each new day on Earth, or anywhere else in the solar system, intentionally start the day with at least twenty minutes of quiet meditation. Take a moment to do some breath work and centre oneself in the belief that One is a special Being in this place – wherever One is now. Align One's mind–body–spirit to resonate with an inner coherence or vibration that unifies One's life energy or 'chi'. Sit in stillness with the irrefutable inner knowing that One is spirit and on an unending journey across the universe. Be the change that One seeks and so it will be in One's life.

One does not need to explain, validate or seek approval for One's spiritual journey or life to others. One only needs to be true to expressing One's infinite existence, so it is in synchronicity with 'the way' of the universe and aligns in harmony with One's spirit. Many people will not be able to come to terms with the fact that One has chosen to spiritually evolve on Earth now. This is because these people have chosen to continue to operate at a lower vibration of existence which is in line with One's ego and egoic programming. It is only when One has lifted the veil of ego within One's own mind that One will be able to see clearly into a new future reality on the planet.

Know that One's human death is only a spiritual doorway back to Source and One's pure consciousness in the universe. There are countless personal stories and individual near-death experiences that support the continued infinite existence of One's spirit, soul or cosmic consciousness. This information is overwhelming and promotes One's spiritual continuity beyond the current concepts of time and space.

What this means is that One is unable to 'conventionally die' as a spirit because One's infinite existence has no 'physical mass' and therefore no 'tangible reality'. It exists within a continuum of unending beingness or non-dimensional realm. One will continue to exist long after One's human form is blowing like ashes in the wind or after the destruction of Earth through the expansion of the Sun into a red giant in this solar system in about five billion years.

Once One has come to the full realisation of One's infinite existence on the planet or place in this solar system, One will begin to see the pointless, senseless and futile egoic governance structures, legislation, laws, policies, programs and projects which are effectively disrupting human spiritual evolution and enabling the destruction of the planet. Successive generations have trained, taught and brainwashed people into various forms of egoic social, cultural and economic slavery. The motivation of this action, which continues in every corner of the world today, is to promote profits over people, separation instead of unity and fear as a go-to substitute for love–peace–harmony. There is also an egoic agenda of control–containment–conditioning as a replacement for free will–freedom–fairness and egoic power rather than spiritual empowerment on the planet.

The good news is that things are continuing to positively change with the rise in people becoming spiritually aware and awake now. In addition, what is also known is that humanity will soon reach a tipping point of individual and collective spiritual realisation that will inevitably change the trajectory of life on the planet for the next thousand years. No matter how hard the egoic elites or egosites of this world try to hold on to One's concentrated wealth, influence and power, it will fail. In fact, the world is already in a state of dismantling the 'old ways' or outdated egoic paradigms of the past.

What will arise is a new way of living, playing, working and being on Earth. Nothing can stop this coming tide of spiritual realisation and collective awakening of people on the planet. It all begins within One now. This is integral to One's infinite existence in the universe. Knowing this gives One certainty in moving forward in life. One has an unshakeable confidence to change anything within oneself and co-create a new interstellar spiritually united Type 1 civilisation on Earth now.

Living as a Being of light, love and oneness

Embracing the idea of living as a sentient spiritual Being is significantly life-changing and possibly very confronting to anyone that has never considered it before now. In simple terms, it enables One to experience the power of manifestation and the joy of living in harmony with the universe. The universe will naturally and effortlessly support One on One's journey to realise and manifest a new, more fulfilling spirit-centric reality and contented spiritual lifestyle on Earth.

> *One must be willing to stand alone – in the unknown, with no reference to authority or the past or any of One's conditioning. One must stand where no One has stood before in complete nakedness, innocence and humility.*
> Adyashanti

The thought of living as a sentient spiritual Being on Earth may be a new concept to many, but it holds great benefits for everyone who chooses to accept it. At its core, living as a Being of light, love, and oneness means imagining and creating a new reality for oneself in the present moment. This requires a shift in perspective, away from the commonly held belief that One is simply a human being having a spiritual experience, to the understanding that One is a spirit, soul, or cosmic consciousness having a human experience.

As a sentient Being, One must take responsibility for One's own spiritual identity and divine sovereignty. This involves recognising that One has come to Earth with a higher purpose now to live as a sentient Being and consciously create One's own reality.

One has the power to intentionally make great changes in One's life today, especially when One aligns with and mindfully focuses One's living energy.

To live a new life on Earth as a sentient Being of light, love and oneness means to imagine a new future for oneself at this present moment. This will most likely be very different from how One was raised and how One is living contemporary life today. It is important to restate that most people on the planet currently believe that One is a human being having a spiritual experience – but this is a false belief. The real truth is that One is spirit, soul or cosmic consciousness expressing itself through a human experience.

> Know that no person, supreme interstellar Being or AI intelligence is coming to save One from oneself in this world. One must accept complete custodianship of One's own spiritual identity and divine sovereignty now.

Learning to live life as a sentient Being on Earth is knowing that One came here with a higher purpose to assist all through the awakening and ascension process to a higher vibration of consciousness on the planet. The simple act of saying 'One is spirit and One is here now' creates a ripple effect in space–time. It also changes the vibrational energy matrix or unified field of potentiality in which One's mind–body–spirit co-exists.

Flipping the script of One's living experiences in the world from a human being who is a receiver of reality to a spiritual Being who is a creator of reality is a dramatic and powerful paradigm shift in One's existence. As One changes the relationship that One has with oneself, One also changes the relationship that One has with other people, places and the world.

In essence, there are three basic modes of operation for all people on the planet:
- victim mode
- survival mode
- creator mode.

This is the natural transition for all people along an enlightenment path and spiritual evolution of all of humanity on Earth.

> *Enlightenment is a destructive process. It has nothing to do with becoming better or being happier. Enlightenment is the crumbling away of untruth. It's seeing through the facade of pretense. It's the complete eradication of everything we imagined to be true.*
> Adyashanti

As One moves through this process, One will enable oneself to go from victim mode (where One feels that things are always out of One's control and unable to do anything about it) to survival mode (where One is solely focused on surviving from day to day and deliberately avoiding pain and suffering in One's life). Finally, One will reach a state of complete acceptance of what is. This is creator mode (where One consciously chooses to manifest how One will experience change, life and a new reality on Earth).

One must make a conscious decision about how One chooses to live life now. Is One going to be a victim, survivor or creator of reality? If One chooses to live life as a sentient Being and create a new reality in this world, congratulations! This is an excellent choice and exciting opportunity in One's life – well done in believing in oneself as a sentient Being of the cosmos. The universe will support One along 'the way' to realise this outcome on Earth. Everything that One does or does not do from this point onwards can be guided by One's spirit to align with One's higher self and greater good in this world.

It is important to realise that nothing is as it seems on Earth. What appears as real is all part of the great cosmic illusion of the universe.

Einstein says, 'Everything in life is vibration.' All is in motion even if One is unable to discern or feel it with One's human senses. Einstein goes on to say, 'Nothing happens until something moves. When something vibrates, the electrons of the entire universe resonate with it. Everything is connected.'

This is why it is so important not to just have the intention to live life as a sentient Being on Earth but to take conscious action to live One's life in a way that honours this divine truth within One's Being. The key to making and manifesting any great change in One's life can be summed up in three simple steps.

Belief

Believe in oneself as a sentient Being of the universe. Believe that One is powerful beyond measure and able to manifest a new reality on Earth with the cooperation of other sentient Beings already here now. Believe in the inherent and intrinsic divine power within One's spirit, soul or cosmic consciousness. Believe that One came to Earth with a purpose to awaken and raise the level of consciousness to a higher level that will enable a new interstellar spiritually united Type 1 civilisation on Earth today.

Intention

Be intentional with One's living energy on this planet and in this solar system. Imagine a new reality and hold it within One's mind as if it already exists or has happened now. Be mindful of the thoughts One thinks, the words One uses to communicate, the behaviours One does, the daily habits One is engaged in, the wellships, partnerships or relationships One is part of and the actions that One undertakes as part of One's life journey. In addition, be mindful of how One conducts oneself at work, play and generally in life. Do no harm to others. Make an effort to connect with other people who align with One's intentional positive energy. Intentionally flow with life and the synchronicity of the universe in every waking moment that One is alive on Earth now.

Action

Take inspired action to realise One's living intention on Earth today. Nothing is achieved without effort and the cooperation of other sentient Beings. Be committed, disciplined and focused in applying One's energy to manifest any imagined outcome. Great change begins with small actions. The world is changed by people who believe in oneself and are committed to creating One's vision for a new reality on Earth. Do not let anyone deter, dissuade or discourage One from One's inner path of enlightenment, self-realisation and awakening as a sentient Being in this world. One's time is limited on this planet, so make the most of every opportunity that is presented to One along 'the way' in this life.

Using this three-step process as a guide will assist One to make changes in One's life and the lives of others on the planet. The world is changing more quickly now. Many people all around the world are moving into a higher level of cosmic consciousness within One's Being. The light of a new reality is becoming more apparent and real as time moves on. Old social structures and egoic paradigms of the past are beginning to dissolve, disappear or collapse. At the same time, new and exciting opportunities are emerging out of this chaos. The answers are coming, but not in ways that One might traditionally think they would.

Many intellectuals, scholars and leaders think technology is the only answer and it will save planet Earth – but it will not. It is only part of the equation. The real answer lies in a global shift in the collective consciousness of every living human being on Earth. To solve the problems of the past, One must use a different level of consciousness that created it in the first place. The way to do this is to live life as a Being of light, love and oneness along with all the other advanced interstellar Beings in the universe.

Creating a shift in collective consciousness

Creating a collective shift in human consciousness is vital for the survival of the human species and the Earth. Individual consciousness directly affects others and it only takes a small percentage of the population to positively influence the rest of the world. The current state of the world is a result of outdated egoic thinking and antiquated systems of governance. This is leading to an increase in living costs and the collapse of key basic functions within families and societies on the planet. The problem with current modern nation-states is that the people living within these collectives or geo-socio-political groupings view the Earth as an endless disposable or throwaway supply of raw materials. This selfish, greedy behaviour has led to a lack of consideration for the planet and future generations. The current trajectory of life on Earth is less than satisfactory, with the possibility of human extinction now looming on the horizon. Global warming and other negative impacts on the climate continue to play a significant part in changing the living landscapes of all humans. The solution is for everyone to change and adopt a spiritual perspective of light, love and oneness, rather than the egoic mindset of greed and materialism. By becoming the change that One seeks, the path to a new future reality on Earth can be created today.

Collective consciousness is a function of individual consciousness. What One does as a Being of light, love and oneness directly affects others in this world. Know that it only takes 1 per cent of the entire population in a state of mind–body–spirit coherence to positively affect the remaining 99 per cent of people living on the planet. This may sound too good to be true, but it is a universal certainty that exists now. It is possible to create a global spiritual harmonic synergy that will change the collective consciousness of everyone everywhere in the world.

It begins with each human being on Earth coming to terms with the truth that One is spirit, soul or cosmic consciousness. One needs to realise that the way forward is not outside but inside oneself. The path to a new future reality on Earth is intrinsically interconnected to the spiritual evolution of each sentient Being alive today.

One may try to run, hide or ignore this truth as much as possible but it is not going away anytime soon. It is an undeniable and inescapable part of One's living reality on the planet.

The growing disruption, uncertainty and dismantling of outdated egoic thinking and systems of governance is a symptom of the changing reality of a shift in consciousness in the world. Most leaders are unclear about how to deal with these changes because these people largely operate from an egoic mindset, framework and doctrine. This type of person is trapped in an unending intergenerational cycle of mindless greed, personal pain and ongoing specific suffering. Old social governance systems, past perspectives and problem-solving strategies that have been used for centuries will not create a new future. The solution is to create a paradigm shift in the collective consciousness of everyone on the planet now.

One has observed that most so-called 'modern' nation-states have adopted a perspective of the Earth as an unlimited consumable resource. This has led to many millions of people using it without regard to One's impact upon it or consideration for future generations. The main driver for most individuals living in contemporary societies has been an egoic attachment within One's mind to money, personal power and material objects. The outcome of this way of life is to selfishly serve oneself. This has been accompanied by the egoic judgement, labelling and separation of people. It is a global practice that separates people into discrete cohorts so that One aligns with specific social groups, categories and types for the benefit of maintaining social control, economic slavery and the status quo of the existing governance systems. This is a well-known practice implemented by all nation-states in the world. Alongside this agenda has been fierce resistance to changing the current way of living, because most people fear losing financial income, housing and food security, quality of life, living relevance and social status in the community.

The relationship between people living in most modern Western governance structures on Earth can be best summarised as 'unconditionally exploitive' with little to no regard for people, place or the planet. This is in direct contrast to First Nations' peoples' relationship with Earth or Country (land, sea and sky), which has a guiding principle of 'respect, honour and custodianship'. There is a fundamental difference in how these two groups of people view One's relationship with Earth or Country.

The Western relationship belief arises out of the egoic concepts of 'greed is good' and 'taking to thrive'. This is all about building and living in a two-way transactional economy without any mutual or collective responsibility for others in the community. The alternative relationship belief is based on spiritual concepts of 'sharing is caring' and 'caring for Country, kin and community'. This is about establishing, maintaining and living in a wellship framework of mutual respect, interconnectedness, personal wellbeing, collective wellness and cultural reciprocity for the benefit of both oneself, others in the community and Country (land, sea and sky).

Earth's habitable biosphere will not survive if the majority of people living on it continue with the egoic practice of being unconditionally exploitive for One's individual selfish gains at the expense of other humans, animals and the planet's natural ecosystems. Egoic personal practices are having a direct effect on the climate of Earth. It is irrefutably changing the landscape in dramatic ways, such as the impact of global warming and rising sea levels along with extreme weather events around the world.

It will soon reach a tipping point where the climate and all life on Earth will be dramatically and adversely affected. The extent of this impact may be such that it might have a negative cascading effect that will lead to the collapse of Earth's habitable biosphere. The Earth's capacity to support humans and all other life on the planet will be significantly reduced. To put it another way, Earth's life support system for humans may be turned off. Human extinction is a real possibility. Everyone everywhere must change and change now.

The good news is that within every sentient Being on the planet exists One's free will to change. To become a Being of light, love and oneness is to be the change that One seeks now. This is the answer that One has been searching for, it is the path that One has been yearning for and 'the way' that One has been dreaming about for a new life on Earth. A life that is filled with great hope, unbounded positivity and overflowing optimism. It exists within all people. One simply needs to take a moment to be still, to listen to One's inner spiritual voice and be guided to the answer. Now is the time to stand up, to be proud, to speak One's truth in a way that celebrates and radiates the light of One's immutable cosmic consciousness to the world.

Go outside wherever One is now and look up at the sky. Take a deep breath and realise that One is intrinsically connected to the universe. This feeling or state of inner oneness exists within One's spirit, soul or cosmic consciousness: today – tomorrow – forever. One is an integral part of the sea of cosmic consciousness in which all interstellar sentient Beings exist.

Know that everything that comes to One in this life will eventually leave as well, so enjoy oneself in the moments that exist now. The way forward is to come together willingly and freely. United in spirit and aligned in harmonic synergy with one another as one collective consciousness on Earth – so be it now.

Activating spiritual intuitive intelligence

Accessing and activating One's spiritual intuitive intelligence is about aligning with One's inner spirit, soul or cosmic consciousness to 'tap into' a state of 'divine knowing'. When One does this it has a significant impact on One's life, decisions, relationships and outcomes, leading to a change in the trajectory of One's living experiences on Earth. Intuitive intelligence, when activated and used properly, leads to a reduction in stress, conflict and suffering. It allows One to flow effortlessly through life. It requires One to surrender from being mind-centred to spirit-centric and involves tapping into Source through One's inner Being. It is an innate ability that exists within every human being and can be rediscovered by practicing compassion. Including spiritual intuitive intelligence in all primary, secondary and tertiary learning curriculums as well as discarding negative cultural beliefs related to low self-worth can help individuals better understand and access their intuitive intelligence.

What is spiritual intuitive intelligence? Intuitive intelligence or divine knowing is more than a spiritual philosophy, 'gut feeling' or applied practice. It exists as part of being in the spiritual state of knowing within One's Being. Some may think it requires a strict training program or needs to be learned over a lifetime, but this is not correct. It is about going within One's inner spiritual consciousness to access a state of 'divine knowing'.

When One begins to operate from this spiritual perspective or life-changing concept, it will naturally have a dramatic effect on One's life, choices, personal connections, direction and outcomes. Over time, it will begin to shape, shift and significantly influence the structure of One's mind–body and life. It will create new connections in the brain, which will give rise to alternative thoughts and emotions. In addition, without realising it, it will simply change the whole trajectory of One's living experiences on Earth.

This change is not to be feared. It is to be embraced and celebrated. One is guided by One's spirit, soul or cosmic consciousness to live a new life that is more aligned with One's higher self. Intuitive intelligence is highly practical when it is applied as part of being compassionate. When One practices the virtue of compassion, it naturally opens a spiritual portal to One's inner state of knowing. In this natural divine state of knowing, it allows One to be completely connected so that information flows freely to oneself. One will be able to sense shifts, ripples and intentions within the fabric of space–time or the unified field of infinite possibilities. In addition, One will begin to see and know the future as if it is all happening at this moment now. This 'conscious knowing' allows One to make good or high-quality, informed choices in One's life. One will be able to choose the most appropriate path to enable the best life outcome at that moment.

Intuitive intelligence, when activated and used properly, will assist One to flow effortlessly and naturally throughout the day or when One is undertaking One's daily tasks. Using One's intuitive intelligence will prevent One from bouncing from one crisis to another. It will also lead One to experience less stress, conflict, pain, suffering and trauma in One's life. Intuitive intelligence is all about being spiritually aware and flowing with the synchronicity of the universe from moment to moment. It is not about avoiding obstacles at any cost, lessening pain and suffering, or getting to One's life destination as quickly as possible. When One is 'in the flow' of the moment, One will realise all One has to do is 'let go' of trying to control the outcome. One will then be naturally guided to where One needs to be. Answers and solutions will simply be revealed to One – yes, it is that simple.

As part of this practice, One will need to surrender from being mind-centred to becoming spirit-centric in how One lives life. One can still be mindful, but One will use One's mind to simply operate the biomechanics of the body to move towards the outcome, solution or destination. This is not a clever game of hide-and-seek that the universe is playing. It is simply 'tapping into' or aligning with Source through One's own inner Being.

The magic of spiritual intuitive intelligence is that it resides in every human being on Earth now. Children generally use it from an early age until One's egoic sociocultural programs or algorithms become more dominant. From the time a human being is born into a modern society, children and young people are immersed in an egoic learning culture where One is taught to be only mind-centred and to disregard, dismiss or deny any learning, knowledge or awareness related to One's spirit, soul or cosmic consciousness. Most people are shamed, ostracised and belittled when the topic of soul, spirit or cosmic consciousness is raised in the classroom, the family, the community or the wider public. There is no curriculum for spirit, soul or cosmic consciousness in public or private schools. It is not considered a valid item for the curriculum and yet it is the single most important issue, topic and subject, and it needs to be included in all classrooms and across all grades in every primary, secondary and tertiary learning institution in the world.

Many people believe in the worthiness of personal pain and suffering in One's life. This type of belief suggests that one must first endure hardships, hate, hurt and harm before One is worthy of self-love or another's affection, kindness or compassion in life. This self-sabotaging self-talk is not true. One is already a divine sentient Being of light, love and oneness and worthy of love, joy and contentment.

One's subconscious programming can often influence One's life for decades. It usually convinces One's mind that suffering is the only path if One is to be taken seriously, be of value to others or earn One's spiritual badge of honour in the universe.

The truth is, as a sentient Being of the universe, One has direct access to the inner state of knowing, which is an integral part of One's consciousness. To be joyful, present, knowing and aware is as natural as the sun shining during the day or the stars twinkling at night. The more One is in One's natural spiritual state, the more One will be able to access and activate One's spiritual intuitive intelligence.

When One is in an internal state of knowing and operating from a place of mind–body–spirit coherence, One is aligned to a specific vibrational frequency that allows One to intuitively tune into life, the universe and everything. It is amazing when One can do this, because it gives One a sense of something greater than oneself and an infinite connection to Source at the same time. One is able to access this ability, power or quality anywhere or any place that One is in the world. It is not conditional on One's gender, race, ethnicity, socioeconomic level, occupation, relationship status, interests, community, location, First Nation or nationality.

But how does One create this situation in One's life today? One can access One's intuitive intelligence by being mindful and spirit-centric about how One chooses to live life at this moment. Intuitive intelligence is not just knowing where One is going or the type of person that One will meet in life. Intuitive intelligence is getting in touch with One's higher self as a creative sentient Being on Earth.

As One continues on One's life journey, One will become aware that the universe is on One's side. It will guide One to a new way of living, working, playing and being on the planet. One's thoughts and feelings of unworthiness, lack of confidence and loneliness will significantly reduce or be removed altogether from One's sense of self.

> One's job is not to 'fight with stress' but to 'flow with life'.

When the mind is still, the whole universe will reveal itself to One in a moment of mindful meditation and spiritual synchronicity.

Know that the universe is supporting One all the time to become a 'Bright' and to reach One's full potential in life. Intuitive intelligence is about operating at a higher vibrational frequency. It enables One to directly access what One really needs to know at this moment. It works best when One can create the right conditions to receive the wisdom, 'the way' and gifts of the universe. When One is committed to activating One's intuitive intelligence, One needs to practice being truly present in the moment.

By using One's intuitive intelligence as a daily habit, One will be able to:
- upskill One's level of intuitive mastery
- increase One's spiritual maturity
- embody inner intuition and sense of knowing as a daily practice
- develop One's spiritual agency to influence change and manifest outcomes
- unconditionally flow along an inner path of spiritual evolution.

Navigating One's spiritual evolution

Navigating One's spiritual evolution is a journey of self-discovery and inner transformation that enables One to experience a deeper connection to and alignment with the universe. It involves embracing a new vision of the future that aligns with a spiritually united Type 1 civilisation on Earth. This will require moving away from ego-driven and individually focused, selfish people and purposely disengaging from these practices and processes in contemporary society. By understanding the power of consciousness and embracing this knowledge, One can evolve as a spiritual Being and experience a more fulfilling, contented and peaceful life.

Humanity's spiritual evolution is the sum of every individual journey of self-exploration and the innermost revolution of One's mind. It is about realising that One is not just a physical human being with a body, but a spiritual entity that exists beyond the human form. This realisation can be challenging, as it can cause One to question One's current long-held beliefs and outlook about the world. It will most likely create a sense of disquiet or considerable distress – this is to be expected. However, it is a necessary process to evolve as a spiritual Being and have a more profound relationship with the universe.

The idea that reality is not what it seems and that One's thoughts and feelings directly influence the world One experiences is a fundamental aspect of spiritual evolution. One has the power to redesign and remodel One's reality by rewriting One's inner thoughts and reforming One's mind–body feelings. This means that One's spiritual path and ultimate evolution are not limited by external circumstances or situations in One's life.

> *Spirituality does not require that you work hard toward achieving a result in the future as much as it requires you to be fully present, sincere and committed now, with absolute honesty and willingness to uncover and let go of any illusions that come between you and the realisation of Reality.*
> Adyashanti

Embracing a new mind–body–spirit coherence that aligns with an interstellar, spiritually united Type 1 civilisation on Earth is a crucial step in One's spiritual evolution. This vision of the future involves moving away from the ego-centric perspective on the planet towards a world of light, love and oneness.

However, many individuals are not yet aware of One's spiritual presence and continue to live life as if One's ego is being operated through some remote control by a third party. This often leads to more stress, pain and suffering, as One tries to force a different outcome with the same old thought paradigm.

Spiritual evolution is not about gaining something or getting somewhere in life. It is simply coming to terms with the divine realisation of oneself as a spiritual entity in the universe. It is realising that One is a Being of light, love and oneness here on Earth now. As One lives life, One is also host to a human form (male, female, transgender or non-binary). This is the sensory bio-machine that interfaces with the 3D world in which One experiences life on the planet.

The idea that One is actually not a human being but a spiritual entity may indeed shake or jolt oneself to think differently about

One's current social habits, numbing addictions, behavioural patterns and subconscious limiting beliefs. This spiritual concept and divine truth will expose One's egoic mind and reveal how it has pulled the wool over One's eyes all this time. If One is humble enough, it may even kick One out of One's 'comfort zone' and spur One to begin a new thought process, challenging all of One's currently held assumptions about life, the universe and everything on this planet.

This new mind–body thought transition will most likely be very uncomfortable for most people. It will inevitably create a sense of great unease and may cause One to experience personal feelings of distress, disruption and possibly despair. These new thoughts and feelings will directly relate to a perception about losing One's old habits, friendship circle, individual personhood, foundation beliefs and living assumptions about oneself and life.

Spiritual evolution is a necessary process to take One beyond what One already thinks One knows. It involves journeying to a new, unknown horizon both in the future and this present moment now. It will challenge One's long-held beliefs and make One face up to One's social and cultural superstitions, perceptions and perspectives from One's past. It will shine a light on the dark areas of One's mind and the hidden agenda of ego.

To evolve as a spiritual Being is to radiate One's divine presence as a 'Bright' in this world and universe. No responsibility is too great and no task is too difficult when One chooses to answer One's inner voice and a spiritual call to action.

The path to the future begins in the present. When One is able to imagine living in the future, it creates the conditions in One's mind as if it is already real and present now. This is how powerful One is as a sentient Being of the universe. What One can imagine directly influences the structure of One's brain. New connections and the rewiring of One's brain is a function of what One dares to imagine now. If One imagines the future as a space where One does not evolve as a spiritual Being – so be it. If One imagines the same future as a space where One evolves into an incredible spiritual Being or 'Bright' – so be it too. Every entity on Earth is a creator of One's own manifested reality and divine future.

> **One's spiritual path and ultimate evolution are not limited by anything in the external world or the conditions in which One lives now.**

Reality today is not what it seems. What One knows or considers to be reality can also be thought of as 'the great illusion', altered consciousness or a unified field of infinite possibilities. All matter arises out of or is manifested from altered consciousness or this infinite unified field. As One reshapes, realigns and reorders this field through One's conscious thoughts and feelings, One reconfigures the right conditions to manifest new and exciting experiences in the world today.

Know that consciousness is pure and precedes all thoughts, feelings and actions in this world. Everything that arises out of matter is a result of previous thoughts and feelings being held within the conscious field of infinite existence first.

To evolve as a spiritual Being is to know this fact and embrace it as part of One's divine existence on Earth today.

If One is aware of One's spiritual presence in this world, why don't others realise the importance of evolving as a Being of light, love and oneness? The main reason that other people have chosen not to evolve is that these individuals are not yet aware of One's spirit, soul or cosmic consciousness. In essence, this type of person is unaware, unawake and still living life with One's ego on autopilot. The future for this type of person is most likely to contain more stress, more pain and more suffering as One tries to use more effort to force a different outcome using the same outdated thought paradigm or ego matrix.

Spiritual evolution involves uploading a new vision for the future. It all begins with embracing a new mind–body–spirit coherence that aligns with an interstellar spiritually united Type 1 civilisation on Earth now. This new vision will enable One to see more clearly and recognise 'the way' forward. One's life will tend to consciously drift away from the horde of mindless masses in the community. One will see that most of the general public still believes in and is driven by One's ego for personal gain, greed and growth. The selfishness of living in an egoic society, witnessing endless waste and observing continual extraction of First Nations' or Earth's resources will have no appeal to One at all.

In understanding this living divergence, One needs to be aware that One is now operating at a different vibrating resonance on Earth. This is why One feels so 'out of sync' with others. It is not because One is 'odd', 'unusual' or even 'eccentric'. It is a result of living life from an alternate spiritual perspective and at a higher mind–body–spirit frequency.

To navigate the best way forward, One must also envision a bridge to the future. It is important that One sees oneself making and creating space for thinking, speaking and doing things in a different way. As One thinks about the path in front of One, take a moment in silent meditation to see all the incremental changes that One needs to flow through along 'the way'.

The bridge to the future is not one giant leap – it is a journey of love, self-care, kindness, harmony, balance, living synchronicity, rest, reflection, healing, nurturing and compassion, just to name a few. It involves managing One's time, thoughts and feelings as well as being disciplined and committed to making incremental changes to One's life while staying focused on the outcome. This begins with a belief in oneself that One is capable of change, has the ability to adapt and is willing to flow in a way that is in One's best interests and higher self.

This may involve:
- planning the night before to manifest the day ahead
- getting up earlier in the morning
- starting the day with a self-check of mind–body–spirit (5–15 minutes)
- exercising every day (30-60 minutes)
- practicing daily mindful meditation and/or manifestation meditation sessions (20–30 minutes, with no electronic devices)

- working on One's individual projects and life goals
- changing One's food intake (e.g. more fresh food, green leafy vegetables, gluten-free and lactose-free meals or keto diet)
- planning for success
- decluttering One's life
- altering One's friendship circle
- taking action to co-create a new living reality in this world
- committing to bringing One's personal best to One's wellships, partnerships and relationships
- raising One's wellness and wellbeing vibration (mind–body–spirit coherence)
- investing in One's wellship with others
- taking time out to just simply be now
- believing and manifesting a new spirit-centric life on Earth today.

Whatever One chooses to change in One's life, be sure that it aligns with One's spirit, soul or cosmic consciousness and flows with the synchronicity of the universe. Stay on the path of spiritual evolution to become a 'Bright' in this life.

Daily affirmation

Use this affirmation to enhance One's way and spiritual life on Earth. Write it down and say it out loud in the morning and before One goes to sleep at night.

One is receiving the blessings of the universe now.

One quickly and effortlessly receives everything One asks for in life.

One's spiritual path and manifestations come to One quickly and effortlessly now.

The universe conspires to help and support One.

Every day One is blessed with miracles and moments of synchronicity.

Great things come to One now.

One is grateful for the love, joy and abundance in One's life.

One is evolving into a 'Bright' – a great and powerful sentient Being of the universe.

IMPORTANT LEARNINGS, TEACHINGS AND POINTINGS

Key ways to live life as spirit, soul or cosmic consciousness

01 The time is now to awaken to the truth of One's infinite existence as spirit, soul or cosmic consciousness in the universe. When One fully embraces and accepts this fundamental truth, an interdimensional portal of spiritual awareness will be opened. This gateway will give One access to inner awareness and an awakened state of spiritual truth and universal wisdom. One will never be able to live life in an unawakened way or 'dream state' on the planet ever again.

02 The key to making and manifesting any great change in One's life can be summed up in three simple steps: belief, intention and action.

03 Together, united and in harmonic synergy as one collective consciousness, is 'the way' forward to a new reality, new spiritual lifestyle and new Earth – so be it now.

04 Know that it only takes 1 per cent of the entire population in a state of mind–body–spirit coherence to positively affect the remaining 99 per cent of people living on the planet. This is a universal certainty that exists now. It is possible to create a global spiritual harmonic synergy that will change the collective consciousness of everyone everywhere in the world.

 When One begins to operate from this spiritual perspective or alternate life-changing concept, it will naturally have a dramatic effect on One's life, decisions, relationships, path and outcomes. Over time, it will begin to shape, shift and significantly influence the structure of One's mind–body (in particular, the connections in One's brain) and life. It will eventually alter the entire trajectory of One's life on Earth.

 Spiritual evolution is not about gaining something or getting somewhere in life. It is simply coming to terms with the divine realisation of oneself as a spiritual entity in the universe. It is realising that One is a Being of light, love and oneness here on Earth now.
The path to the future begins in the present. When One is able to imagine living in the future, it creates the conditions in One's mind as if it is already real and present now. Reality today is not what it seems. What One knows or considers to be reality can also be thought of as 'the great illusion', altered consciousness or an energetic field of infinite possibilities.

PART FOUR

Transform One's mind-body-spirit coherence

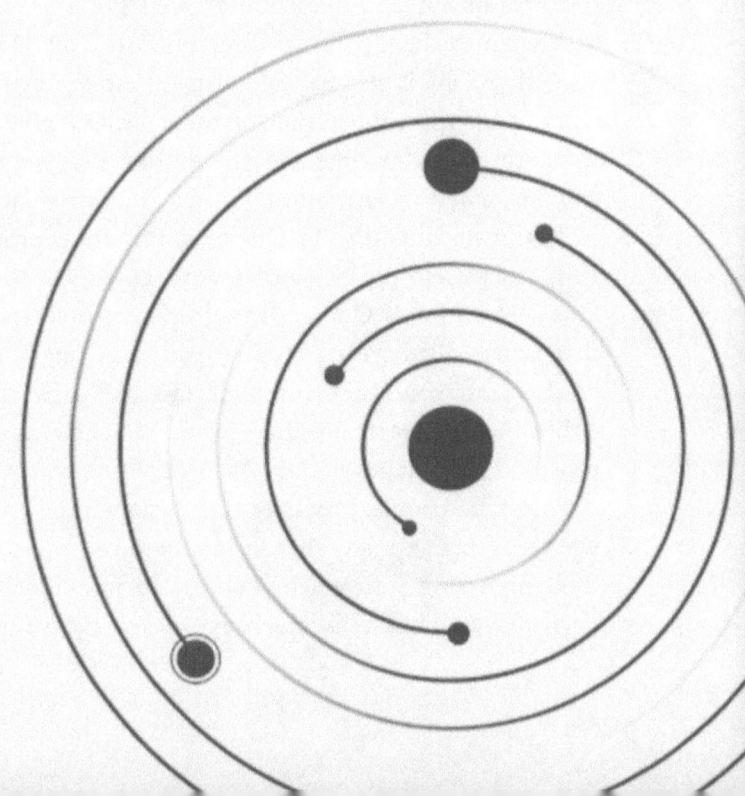

Creating a new mindful vision and conscious reality

The significance of creating a new mindful vision and conscious reality of an interstellar spiritually united Type 1 civilisation on Earth is of utmost importance if humanity is to spiritually evolve within this galaxy. In a world that is constantly changing and evolving, it is essential for every individual to take a step back and reflect on One's own life.

If One seeks a new life in this world, One needs to imagine a new vision for oneself. The sooner One changes the way that One observes or looks at oneself and One's life on Earth, the sooner it will begin to change in that direction. After all, One is a creator of One's life. One is also capable of manifesting any experience in the world with the cooperation of other sentient Beings. One simply needs to invest the time and energy to reimagine how it may look and feel, and how energetically it may be experienced now.

To transform One's life, One must first transform oneself (mind–body–spirit). To put it another way, 'One must be the change that One seeks now'. If One desires a different life experience on Earth that is not filled with continual pain and ongoing suffering, One needs to awaken One's consciousness to a new way of living life. A life that is free from One's egoic attachments, judgements and resistance to changes within One's mind–body.

For some people, breaking this cycle will be hard but for those who are 'change ready' it will be a natural transition. There is no right or wrong path when it comes to individual transformation. Each person must seek 'the way' that is right for One, wherever

One is and in a direction that best suits One at this moment of One's life.

Know that the negative thoughts and feelings of One's past are not required for the future. One needs to leave it all behind. In fact, it will be necessary to purge oneself of this accumulated energy and biological imprint. To do this, imagine the thoughts and feelings of a new and beautiful life, partner, friendships or experiences as if they are real now. The brain does not know the difference between 'imagined reality' and 'real life'. To it, it is all the same, it is just the reality that One chooses to believe at this moment.

> *Your perception of the world is a reflection of your state of consciousness.*
> Eckhart Tolle

Know that, to the universe, 'all reality' is virtual. When One creates a new mindful image in One's mind, it forms new neural synapses and rewires the scaffolding of the brain into an alternative network. As One creates and uses this new positive pattern, it branches out to create even more connections, reshaping and reconfiguring the physical matter of the brain from within. This is how new positive thoughts and feelings alter the structure of the brain and the overall vibrating frequency of One's mind–body–spirit.

This means that every person on Earth can change One's neural networks within the brain using mindful meditation, altered thinking-speaking and creative consciousness – changing the present by believing in a new future that is positive, uplifting and overflowing with optimism.

> What One believes – One imagines.
> What One imagines – One creates within One's mind and then can manifest it in the 'real world'.

One will intuitively know if One is living a 'fake or false life' now. It will feel essentially empty, as if One is simply going through the motions of work–rest–sleep. One may even feel like One is in a never-ending cycle, doing the same things over and over again without ever achieving a real or tangible life outcome. It will seem like One is drifting from day to day and moment to moment without a real sense of getting ahead or going anywhere in life. The sign that One is living a mindless and meaningless life is when One realises that One's energy is being wasted, without any real focus, purpose or being in the 'now' of One's spiritual existence. A good indicator of this is when 'activity does not equal or contribute to an outcome'. One may question One's job, One's purpose and One's life on the planet. One may even ask: 'What is the purpose of everything?' 'What does it all mean'?

To have doubt is a good sign and the first crack in One's egoic mental matrix or conditioned cognitive framework. It means One is beginning to question how One is choosing to live life on Earth.

> **For every question, there is an answer in the world. For every problem, there is a solution in the universe too.**

The truth of One's spiritual or conscious existence cannot be hidden from oneself long. It is within One. It has and will always be within One now.

Knowing this truth will enable One to set oneself free. Free of the sociocultural conditioning of One's past, free of the expectations of others, free of the traps of relationship guilt and unworthiness, free of being in debt, free of living up to someone else's ideals, free from the impact of perceived judgement of others, free of the need for people to validate One's spiritual identity and sovereignty as a divine sentient Being of the universe.

When One finally realises that One is free, it will feel as if a great weight has been lifted from One's shoulders or a dark cloud has been removed from One's life. One can finally breathe fresh air again and fill One's lungs with a great sense of hope, faith and trust.

When something ends in One's life, it usually means that a new beginning is about to start. This is how the universe works. It is all part of the ebb and flow of cosmic life in space and time. It is important to celebrate and honour the passing of people in One's life, because these individuals will not be here forever. Everyone and everything has its time and place in this world.

Know that One's time and energy are limited on Earth. One's mind–body has about one hundred Earth revolutions of the Sun as a living human being to experience this world before the deconstruction and dematerialisation of One's DNA. One hopes that this might inspire some urgency in One's life. It is anticipated that it will also motivate One to prioritise One's precious life on the planet and invest in things that will create change to benefit oneself, others and future generations.

Do not surrender One's mind–body, spirit and life mindlessly to others or systems of organised manipulation and control that will reduce One's life to a functional unit of energy or transhuman existence on the planet. Take the time to reimagine it into something beautiful, amazing and wonderful now. Create a new mindful vision and conscious reality that has at its core some key ideas, concepts, models, practices, suggestions and quality attributes, such as:

- an interstellar spiritually united Type 1 civilisation on Earth
- connected collective consciousness on the planet
- spiritual intuitive intelligence practised in all communities
- mindful, virtuous and spirit-centric living
- loving, harmonious and mutually respectful wellships, partnerships and relationships
- prosperous, abundant and awakened life experiences for all
- interstellar travel and contact with other living entities in the galaxy
- free zero-point or quantum field energy on the planet for everyone everywhere

- global use of the 'language of Spirit or One'
- free access to all education for all citizens of Earth
- universal Earth citizenship for every person born on Earth
- universal health care for everyone on the planet
- worldwide digital currency that is based on social utility, global inclusiveness, human rights and basic living requirements
- planetary peace, harmony and balance within families, communities, societies, First Nations and the world (i.e. an Earth without wars or violence)
- human beings living in synchronicity with spirit and all life forms
- a planet that is healed and restored to its natural beauty.

The key to co-creating this new vision is to first believe in it now. What comes next is the path of realisation as One's divine consciousness streams forward to manifest this new reality out of altered consciousness or the energetic unified field of infinite possibilities. Simply believe, plan and act in alignment with this reality – so it will be now.

Accessing One's infinite potential and cosmic consciousness

Accessing One's infinite potential and cosmic consciousness is a concept that encourages individuals to tap into One's inner power and connect with One's divine consciousness. This leads to a more enjoyable, rewarding and transformative life experience, as One realises One's true worth, infinite potential and becomes an agent of change in the world.

This idea has been gaining more popularity in recent times. It is a belief that suggests each individual has the transformative capacity to unlock an inner way to totally change and enable a new life experience or awakened way of living life on Earth.

The journey to accessing One's limitless possibilities begins with self-awareness, self-realisation and self-love. It is crucial to recognise that One is a special and unique Being, with powers beyond measure. Learning to love oneself unconditionally is key to unlocking access to divine consciousness within. Every human thought and feeling creates a specific energy field in One's life. One must learn to control and manage One's thoughts and feelings to cultivate this divine power.

It is also important to accept that One is an activator of alternative realities, with the capability to affect the energy field within One's mind–body–spirit and completely change the world around oneself too. This can be achieved through mindful actions and applied consciousness practice, such as meditation. Believing in One's infinite potential and worthiness is crucial to transforming One's life and becoming a Being of light, love and oneness.

One must align or 'get in touch' with One's real Being. This means creating time and space to simply be present now. By living in the moment, One can also become a Being of great joy, unconditional love and a wonderful gift to the world.

Wherever One's focus goes, One's energy flows. This can be positive, high-vibrational energy or negative, low-vibrational energy in One's life. The choice is up to One when actioning or expressing One's intent in the world to achieve any life outcome.

The first step in accessing One's infinite potential is knowing of its existence within oneself now. Know that One is an indomitable spirit with powers beyond measure in this world. One may have never been told that One is special when One was a child. Remind oneself now. One is special, unique and an integral part of the universe. As a sentient Being of light, love and oneness, know that One is not alone in the universe – One never has been and never will be.

Learning to unconditionally love oneself is key to unlocking One's access to an alternative stream of divine consciousness within oneself. One, as much as anybody in this world, is worthy of One's love, affection and attention. Whatever One focuses on in life, One is directing both One's own life force or 'chi' energy as well as the energy of the universe into this space.

One is both a creator and an enabler of change. Depending on One's perspective and what One thinks, these changes can be seen as either 'good' or 'bad'. One can either be moving more in alignment with One's spirit, soul or cosmic consciousness or further away from it. Whatever One chooses in life, know that energy does not lie – it is always truthful. One's energy introduces oneself to all before One even speaks. This is why when One meets a new person for the very first time, One will automatically feel or sense this individual's energy without ever speaking to this person. One will 'get a vibe' if this new person is radiating good, peaceful, calm, loving, kind, positive high energy or bad, angry, restless, hateful, unkind, negative low energy. The distinction between these two types of energy fields emanating from anybody will be obvious to the average person.

Animals and creatures in the wild are very sensitive to the energy of other entities. They can read or interpret it far more accurately than human beings. This is because they are intuitively connected to this unified energy field all the time. Animals use it to detect intent and determine if other animals or human beings are a threat to One's life or survival. Before any action is initiated by another animal or human being, there is a quantum shift in the conscious unified energy field that aligns with this intent and action. Although it may not be able to be measured in any empirical terms, this quantum shift is nonetheless very real and very noticeable when One is attuned to it.

Hence, One must be very mindful when selecting One's intentions at any moment of the day. Every conscious thought and feeling sets up a specific energy field. This is why One is not just a passive person living in the community and sharing the world. One is actually an 'agent of change', and can affect the unified field within and around oneself simply with One's presence in this world.

> **Being present impacts everyone and everything in life.**

One must learn and train One's mind to select One's thoughts and feelings the same way One would purposely choose a meal and drink from a menu when dining out. One is able to access this inner quality and cultivate this power through mindful meditation and conscious practice. If One seeks to manage things in One's life, first manage One's thoughts and feelings (emotions) within oneself.

One is not responsible for what others may think of oneself. Especially if One decides to choose to be a different person, live an alternative lifestyle or simply have an unconventional belief about oneself, life and the universe. One is under no obligation to be the same person when One was born, or five minutes ago or five years ago. This means that One needs to accept people where One is in life. This is best achieved when One does not attach any particular meaning to another person's story, experience or journey. All One has to do is accept what is at this moment.

Believing in One's infinite potential is at the core of accepting One's inner capacity and capability to completely transform oneself and One's life today. Realise that One is truly worthy, One is particularly valuable and One is incredibly special. One has an important purpose on Earth and thus, by implication, One is on a significant life journey as a spiritual Being now. Do not let anyone else convince One otherwise. Living life as a spirit, soul or cosmic consciousness is an expression of the universe itself.

Never be scared of experiencing silence, being by oneself or accessing the divinity of One's cosmic consciousness. After all – this is who One truly is.

Sometimes it will be particularly important to distance oneself from others to get in touch with the real 'isness' of One's Being. Be sure to make time and create space as part of regular mindful meditation practice to just sit in stillness, listen in quietness and receive in gratefulness all that will come to One.

> **Silence is 'the way' to spirit, soul or cosmic consciousness and other interstellar entities in the universe.**

Do not be in a hurry to race through life or get to the next great thing on offer in the world. All that is meant for One will come soon enough. Take time to live in the moment now. Be a Being of great joy, with great love and a great gift to share with others and the world. For every door that closes in One's life, many more will open. Just be present now in this space.

Know that the greatest periods of darkness and loss in One's life can often produce the brightest moments of inspiration, light and awakening. Being grateful for One's infinite potential is a sign that One is appreciative of this quality within oneself.

Many people do not want to hear the truth about being a Being of light, love and oneness because it will destroy One's illusion about oneself in this world. The more One tries to escape One's divine spiritual destiny in life, the more obstacles One will encounter to nudge One back on track to align with One's higher self today. The universe does not have some grand plan to make One's life hard, difficult or challenging. It is simply there for One. Have patience for all things in life and especially with oneself and others. Because One exists now at this moment in time, One is enough. Know this truth now and be content with One's inner spiritual Being and life on Earth today.

It is never too late to change One's mind, beliefs and direction in life. One is not the product of One's past decisions or a prisoner of One's current perception. One is so much more than this. Look beyond these shallow interpretations of life and ask oneself a different question. Go deep and make a personal inquiry of oneself. Ask:

- *What does One's best-fulfilled life look life, feel and sound like?* Imagine it now, write it down, take note of what this alternative reality is. Hold this vision within One's mind and

take inspired action towards manifesting the right conditions to realise this outcome in One's life today.
- *What does One need to change in order to transform One's life now?* Know that the answer will come to One – then go out and commit to manifesting this experience in the world today.

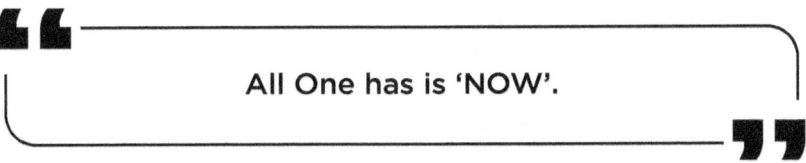

All One has is 'NOW'.

Seven keys to personal empowerment and transformation

There are many ways to shift One's inner energy and create outer changes in One's life. Some strategies can fix an issue, concern or worry in the short term and others have lasting, long-term benefits. The more One can create a change within One's consciousness field of existence, the more One will be able to dramatically manifest a new reality in the world today.

Most people on the planet seek to make the world a better place, particularly if one has a family and is looking out for the family's and community's future or best interests. But sadly, a lot of people, parents and partners feel trapped in One's own fear and believe that One is unable to escape it. This is because many individuals are caught in an egoic cycle of mindless doing. This involves acting without care or concern for self and others, thinking without being mindful of One's life and its impact on the planet, and living life without any spiritual awareness and being an integral part of the universe now.

Through a new conscious awareness of One as spirit, soul or cosmic consciousness, One is able to rewrite One's life story on the planet. As One changes the script of One's life to align with a new version of oneself, this new story will also rewire One's brain and neural networks too. One can then experience One's inner Being, life, events, activities, relationships and moments in a more meaningful and purposeful way. This fundamental paradigm shift will enable a new reality. A life that will create more joy, harmony, balance, synchronicity, peace, love, knowing, awareness, creativity, light and oneness as One journeys through this life.

When One realises that One is in charge of One's empowerment process, One will also need to take personal responsibility for it. One cannot outsource One's own transformation to somebody else in the hope that this person will do a better job. This will always end in failure, because One is using hope as an empowerment strategy and it never works. Hoping that something external changes in One's life to automatically transform oneself into a better person, lover, partner, individual, worker, family and community member or citizen is pointless. It is never going to happen. One must be One's own inner change agent and captain of One's ship of destiny now.

Know that there is no guarantee in life. All relationships are impermanent and life on Earth is filled with inescapable uncertainty. In response to this, One must simply embrace it face-on as it is happening at the moment. Surrender to what is now. Do this without any expectation or entitlement for anything in this world. From this point, One can begin to move forward in any direction that aligns with One's spirit, soul or cosmic consciousness, in sync with the universe.

There are seven keys to personal empowerment and transformation that One can use as a guide to change oneself, One's life and create a new trajectory towards a better life outcome.

> **Seven keys to personal empowerment and transformation**
>
> 1. Awaken to spirit, soul or cosmic consciousness within oneself
> 2. Believe in oneself as a sentient Being of the universe
> 3. Create a clear new vision of the future
> 4. Act with proactive intent, genuine honesty and spiritual integrity
> 5. Be present in every living moment in life
> 6. Flow in coherence, cooperation and co-existence with all
> 7. Live life as a spiritual and mindful practice now

Key 1: Awaken to spirit, soul or cosmic consciousness within oneself

Principle: One realises who One truly is in the universe.

The first key to personal empowerment and transformation is to achieve clarity about who One truly is in this life, world and universe. What flows from this realisation is that One is not a human being but a divine sentient Being hosting a human form (male, female, transgender or non-binary). As One discovers One's own divine identity and cosmic sovereignty, it will create a paradigm shift in One's reality and place on this planet. One will not be able to view oneself the same way ever again. Billions of people are going about One's daily life on Earth with the view that One is human – this is not correct. This hand-me-down story mistakenly informed people of a false truth which was perpetrated through countless generations until today. One needs only to look inside oneself to see the truth of One's existence in this world so that One can create an alternate narrative that speaks to One's heart and higher self. It is time to tell oneself this new story as a sentient Being of light, love and oneness as often as possible throughout the day.

It is enough for One to know that One simply exists now. Nothing needs to be added or subtracted from One's spirit for it to be perfect – One already is.

Key 2: Belief in oneself as a sentient Being of the universe

Principle: One knows with inevitable certainty of
One's infinite existence as an indomitable spirit and
that One is powerful beyond measure.

The second key is to believe in oneself not as a human being having a spiritual experience but as a spiritual Being experiencing being host to a human form. When One realises that One exists as a divine entity in the cosmos. Amazing things begin to happen and appear automatically in One's life. This belief is at the centre of One's existence in the universe. One will naturally be able to sense a 'real truth' to One's life and living presence on the planet. It will create great spiritual confidence in oneself and this confidence will activate an increased amount of inner commitment to simply being oneself. This, in turn, will promote a higher level of spiritual competency in Being what One knows One is now – a sentient Being of the universe.

In short, this inner belief will create spiritual confidence – which will increase spiritual commitment – that will then promote higher spiritual competency in life. At the end of this cycle, it will create a feedback loop that will enable more spiritual confidence and so on and so forth. Everything will expand from within oneself moving forward.

Key 3: Create a clear new vision of the future

Principle: One's vision of the future precedes all
creation and manifestation of any new reality or
experiences in One's life.

The third key is to imagine a new reality as if it is already present now. Practice visualising oneself living a new life with new experiences as if it has already happened. Feel all the thoughts and feelings of this new manifested reality as if One was living it today. Connect with One's inner consciousness and shift One's own energetic field of infinite possibilities to align with this new vision. Do this practice every day. Know that whatever One thinks about the most is what One is investing One's creative energy in now.

Here are three easy steps to help One get started.

Create a vision board or vision workbook or manifestation diary

What does One seek to experience in this new reality? Capture all of One's thoughts and feelings in words or pictures – what best describes the energy of this future, not necessarily the exact things.

Develop a manifestation map

How will One build a bridge to this new reality? Identify practical pathways and a sense of effortless energy to create the right conditions that will take One towards this new living outcome.

Make a partners plan

Who will share One's journey to make this vision a new reality? List the most likely cooperative relationships or supportive partnerships that One will need to engage, establish and enable.

Make a conscious effort to begin each day, task, or project with a clear vision of One's desired direction, final destination and divine destiny. Then flow with mindful virtuous energy and meaningful action to make it happen. Prime oneself for success in the morning by changing, altering or reconfiguring One's life.

- Wake up and get up early.
- Exercise.
- Practise mindful meditation.
- Affirm that One is a spiritual Being with an important purpose and mission on Earth.
- Focus on the vision as if it is a manifested certainty in life.
- Be intentional and proactive with One's thoughts, feelings, words, speech, habits and actions throughout the day.
- Express with deep gratitude the benefits of this new future reality to oneself and others in the real world.
- Learn to play the long game or engage in infinite game theory by using an ongoing continuity perspective to be always flowing in play, success, business or life.
- Know that One is a leader of One's own life and must take full responsibility for oneself and this vision of the future.
- Believe that One has infinite potential to co-create One's own destiny today.
- Simply just do it – invest One's life energy to ensure the future One envisions now.

Key 4: Act with proactive intent, genuine honesty and spiritual integrity

Principle: One is free to choose One's path and experiences so that they align with One's spirit and are in synchronicity with the universe.

The fourth key is to cultivate a practice that creates conscious awareness of One's intentions as well as a deep connection to One's genuine honesty and spiritual integrity throughout the day.

To stay connected to One's intentions and not revert back to One's old subconscious social conditioning and cultural programming of the past, One must learn to manage One's mental, physical and emotional energy at every moment of the day. This involves positively focusing on the thoughts, feelings and emotions that will support One in achieving One's identified intentions, tasks and life goals. Whatever needs to be done first – just do it now. Like a pebble skipping across the water, every step begins as part of an interconnected series of events and actions in motion. Move One's mind–body–spirit so that it flows like water down a stream – effortless and easy. Nature does not rush and yet everything in life is stunning, beautiful and overflowing with abundance.

Stay centred within One's Being as One goes about One's daily tasks, activities and projects. Let no person disturb One's inner peace and sense of spiritual identity. Always bring One's virtuous habits, positive vibrations and spiritual authenticity into the space that One is in now. Do what works and work on what needs to be done first – simplicity is the key to creating solutions to any complex issue, concern or worry.

Key 5: Be present in every living moment in life

Principle: One exists in an unending sea of cosmic consciousness, divine relationships and a unified field of infinite possibilities. Everything is One – all is connected.

The fifth key is being present in life by acknowledging that One co-exists within an energetic unified field of infinite possibilities with other sentient Beings of the universe. One is not here in competition, One is here to cooperate with other entities in the cosmos. This means that One must create space and time to honour One's own spirit and the spirit of other people in the world when One is engaging with these individuals. One does this by listening in silence and from a place of openness. Be non-judgemental when One is communicating with others on Earth. Remember that One is engaging through One's mind–body–spirit, not just responding to what someone else says.

Communication is key to all great relationships in this world. These relationships all form part of a spiritual journey which is about working in harmony with others, including interstellar Beings, in a way that flows in synchronicity with the universe.

There are three ways of looking at collaborative relationships:
- 1 + 1 = 2 (this way or that way – only two options available)
- 1 + 1 = 3 (this way or that way or a fusion of both ways (e.g. win–win) – only three options available)
- 1 + 1 = ☐ (window) (this way or that way or infinite ways of the universe or possibilities or options available because of quantum spiritual entanglement)

As One ceases operating from an ego-centred framework and consciously chooses to live life from a spirit-centric perspective, amazing and wonderful things begin to happen in One's life. One realises that there is enough for all citizens on the planet to live in harmony, peace, love, prosperity and abundance. The more One gives, the more there is to share. One's cup will be full if people simply gave what One can to others with the intention of creating a better life, community and world. This is all part of the spiritual evolution of humanity moving forward to embrace an interstellar spiritually united Type 1 civilisation on Earth now.

Key 6: Flow in coherence, cooperation and co-existence with all

Principle: One moves with 'the way' of the universe – without expectation, attachment, judgement or resistance to change.

The sixth key is to flow in harmony and synchronicity with One's spirit and 'the way' of the universe. It is about being open to new options, ideas and solutions that do not repeat the same dysfunctional unconscious mindless patterns of the past. It is acknowledging that One needs to let go of One's ego and leave it at the door of opportunity and innovation. Creating innovative solutions increases exponentially when One aligns with One's spirit and taps into the consciousness field of infinite possibilities. The only limits are those that each individual person places on oneself.

Flowing with grace and ease in a state of 'no-mind' or Zen-like meditation is possible when One is not attached to anything and accepts everything at this moment. When people realise that One can either be part of the problem or the solution and consciously choose to shift One's mental (thoughts) and physical (feeling) energy to operate in this way, it creates a synergy for new and powerful solutions in life and on the planet.

As One realises that life is a journey of expressed consciousness and different vibrating energies within each person, One will begin to appreciate One's ability to influence the stream of One's own spiritual consciousness and thus the world in which One lives now. Know that One has the power to reshape, reorganise and reconfigure One's mind–body–spirit, life and world into any new reality or future manifestation that One chooses.

Key 7: Live life as a spiritual and mindful practice now

Principle: One incorporates virtuous and conscious daily habits that support One's mind–body–spirit wellness, wellship and wellbeing. One consciously commits One's life energy to spiritually evolve as a 'Bright' - an awakened Being in the universe. As part of this living destiny, One chooses to co-create with other sentient Beings a new interstellar spiritually united Type 1 civilisation on Earth now.

The seventh key is to make One's life a living spiritual practice by incorporating virtuous habits into every aspect of One's life. This means applying the seven key virtues – compassion, helpfulness, acceptance, generosity, simplicity, patience and openness – in whatever task, work or project that One is undertaking. As One is practising the virtue of generosity, One can be grateful for the opportunity to give and receive from others and the universe. This naturally opens a spiritual gateway to One's spirit and Source. One is able to tap directly into the consciousness or quantum field to effect change through aligning One's presence with a new manifested intention. This creates change from within, which influences the reality of the world or space and time that One currently occupies.

As One chooses to consciously change, One will also mindfully choose to change the language, words and speech that One uses to align more with the intention of living in harmony and balance with One's spirit and the natural flow of the universe. Shifting One's perception and language will naturally alter the neural pathways in the brain to align with One's higher self. One will be literally rewiring One's brain to vibrate at a higher level, which is all part of the evolution process for human beings on the planet.

Renewing, reimagining and reaffirming One's infinite existence as a sentient Being of the universe creates profound changes in One's life. These changes will include an upgrade to One's living operating system and the mind–body physical reconstruction of One's living human form on the planet. Some changes will be subtle, while others will be dramatic shifts in One's perception, awareness and presence.

As One's coherent mind–body–spirit energy begins to vibrate at a higher level, One will find oneself living life more in sync with the natural rhythm of the universe and distancing oneself from negative low energy people, activities and events. Do not be alarmed. This is all part of One's evolving process towards a new reality on Earth now.

Developing One's spiritual toolbox for life

Life is an opportunity to live, grow and simply be in this world. Often the beauty of living well, loving with gracefulness, receiving and giving with gratitude or just being joyful in life can be challenged by One's interpersonal relationships, work–life priorities or daily tasks. Know that life was never meant to be lived in a straight line. Neither was it meant to be filled with constant hardships, stress and fears. Somewhere among all these human experiences One needs to stop and ask oneself a different question: How does One change One's life and lifestyle right now to be in coherence with One's mind–body–spirit and aligned to One's higher self or divine consciousness?

When One takes the time to ask a different question, it sets up a different relationship with oneself and the universe at that moment. It also changes the trajectory of One's life on the planet. This simple act is a powerful expression of One's inner Being and the foundation for developing One's spiritual toolbox for life.

What is a spiritual toolbox? A spiritual toolbox is a personal resource of wellness, wellship and wellbeing ideas, strategies, actions, practices and habits that One can use when feeling challenged in life. One may already be using some 'go to' approaches that work for oneself now. There are other suggestions that may be completely new to One's way of living in this world too. A spiritual toolbox typically contains things like taking time to be in nature, mindful meditation, gentle exercise, spiritual habits, virtue practices, breath work training, writing and journalling about One's aspirations, thoughts and ideas, spending time with good supportive friends and self-care (e.g. spa bath or massage, giving oneself a special treat, reading a good book or maybe just even some quiet time alone).

The list of what One puts in One's spiritual toolbox is endless but the outcome is the same: being in alignment with a state of coherent resonance within One's mind–body–spirit. Living in this inner state of coherence from a place of One's higher self wherever One is on Earth.

A spiritual toolbox is much more than positive suggestions or a feel-good bucket list. It is preventative medicine that will promote wellness in One's life. When One engages in this type of lifestyle, it has the power to transform One's life completely. Not in a small way, but in big ways that create a dynamic shift in One's living energy and spiritual consciousness. One knows that adapting, adjusting and affirming wellness practices and mindful habits on a daily basis will result in positive changes to One's overall life and lifestyle. One will think more clearly, have more energy, experience less stress, feel more at peace within oneself, be socially connected and generally have better health. One will realise that the best way to create the life experiences that One seeks is to learn how to reorganise, reprioritise and recommit to exactly the way One chooses to live life on the planet now.

A spiritual toolbox overflows with practical approaches to support One in living a mindful life and spiritually conscious existence on Earth. A way that will extend One's life on the planet where One will be content, radiate joy, emanate gratitude, shine with lightness, go with grace, respond with humility and positively transform One's life into a beacon of wisdom and wellness.

Everything that One aspires to in life is possible with a loving spirit, kind heart, an open mind and a vision of the future where One is free of egoic fears and false truths in this world.

One's spiritual toolbox may include:
- be spiritually in sync
- adapt, evolve and innovate
- be realistic, relevant and reflective
- continually improve oneself (mind–body–spirit)
- be aware and open to everything
- listen, learn and live life now
- be accepting and giving to all.

Be spiritually in sync

Learning to love oneself as spirit, soul or cosmic consciousness is key to inner and outer change in One's life. It is also a way to know the universe too. Every moment of every day that One is alive on Earth, realise that One is a spiritual Being experiencing life through a human form. Create space in One's life to meditate in silence and align in sync with One's spirit and the universe. Expand One's consciousness out into the world and beyond. Reach inwards to know oneself now. One is the key to creating new relationships with oneself and others.

> *Love and compassion are necessities, not luxuries. Without them, humanity cannot survive.*
> His Holiness the 14th Dalai Lama

As One spiritually evolves, One will open a divine doorway for oneself and others in this world. Living in sync is as easy as breathing when One is consciously aware of One's infinite existence in this world. With every step, breathe; with every moment, be now.

Adapt, evolve and innovate

Life is change – change is life. One is not the same person that One once was at the age of ten, twenty, thirty or forty. Things change and so do people. Adapting to life is an important part of developing, growing and changing One's human form and thoughts on the planet. One needs to constantly upgrade One's living operating system or thought processes to align with One's higher spiritual self in this world. Just because One grew up in a certain way with a particular culture, using a distinct language within a unique social group or First Nation or community does not mean that One is locked into those memes for life. One has a choice. A choice to let go of past attachments and judgements so One can change and be the best version of oneself now.

> *Letting go gives us freedom, and freedom is the only condition for happiness. If, in our heart, we still cling to anything – anger, anxiety, or possessions – we cannot be free.*
> Thich Nhat Hanh

One is on a spiritual evolutionary journey whether One realises it or not. One's past is not present and neither is One's future. One must learn to rise above the negative vibrations of One's ego and go beyond the illusion of reality in front of One's eyes now. It is time to embrace One's spiritual life on the planet. Become the master of One's thoughts, feelings and actions. Do this by continually adapting, evolving and innovating oneself each and every day that One is alive on Earth.

Be realistic, relevant and reflective

Life is not about doing more; it is about being in the moment when One is living life. One can aim for the stars, but One must also be grounded in where One is now. It is okay to have dreams. Dreams are a place where One can imagine a different future and living experiences. Dreams can inspire people to do some amazing things in life. They can also show or reveal to One an alternative way to look at or live life in the present moment too. The thing about dreams is that One still needs to build a bridge to this future reality. Pleasure and satisfaction are found most often not in arriving at the destination but in realising the journey along the way.

> *We realise – often quite suddenly – that our sense of self, which has been formed and constructed out of our ideas, beliefs and images, is not really who we are. It doesn't define us, it has no center.*
> Adyashanti

Keeping it real and relevant is key to realising any vision that One imagines that relates to oneself, meeting new people, exploring new places or being immersed in new experiences. It takes space and time in One's life to reflect on where One would like to be and why. Why is it so important that One does what One is doing now? What is the meaning of going this way or that way? What if One simply chose to be now? Be still and allow the answer to come to One.

Continually improve oneself (mind-body-spirit)

'From little things, big things grow.' Whichever path One has chosen to take in life, learn how to continually improve oneself (mind-body-spirit) along 'the way'. The better that One gets at reading the signs of self-improvement, the quicker One will be able to progress through all of One's life lessons. Know that everyone is One's teacher and One is Master to all. Look for opportunities to rise above the ordinary by serving others in an extraordinary way. One does not have to be like everyone else on the planet. One is unique and special. One has amazing gifts, skills and abilities to bring and share with the world. One simply needs to figure out what those things are and shine a light on them so that it can light One's way and others to a better future on this planet.

Andrew Newberg and Mark Robert Waldman say: 'The simple act of watching your own consciousness actually improves your mood, your self-esteem, and your overall satisfaction with life. Research also shows that self-reflective observation and awareness activates structures in the brain directly associated with enlightenment and transformation.'

Continuity of creative improvement begins with the idea and a belief in oneself. One is capable of great change and can express this greatness through One's mind–body–spirit. Create a level of confidence that 'One has got this' and commit to improving oneself not in leaps and bounds but through regular, incremental steps each and every day. If One wants to be good at something, do it for one or two hours every day. After a year, One will have invested hundreds of hours of training to improve oneself. After five years, One will have become a high-performing individual or expert in the field with thousands of hours of investment in oneself. Self-investment is the key to self-improvement: today – tomorrow –always.

Be aware and open to everything

'One leaf – same tree.' 'Many paths – one way.' Know that there are many ways that One can take in life to arrive at the same destination. One simply needs to remain open to everything and reject nothing along 'the way'.

> When we become spiritually aware – through synchronicity, for example – it's a sign that despite the uncertainty, we are aligned with the force of life.
> Lisa Miller

Create an inner awareness of One's wellness (mind–body–spirit) and choose the path that best suits One's personal wellships or individual wellbeing. Stay centred within One's spirit and allow all the options to simply wash over One now. Do not choose the fastest or most convenient way forward. Choose what 'feels good' and is the best fit for One's healing or wellness path in life.

Go with the flow of life and let life flow within One now. One has the power to heal One's mind–body through mindful wellness meditation, positive thinking, healthy living-eating-being, self-belief and reconfiguring One's own quantum field of divine consciousness to manifest an alternative life or living experiences in the world.

Choose to be aware of One's own infinite existence and what this means as a living sentient Being in life. Choose wellness. Choose life.

Listen, learn and live life now

Take care to connect and align with One's spirit. Learn to listen in silent meditation as part of One's daily habits when One begins each new day. Create space for quiet time at the beginning of the day, throughout the day and at the end of the day too. Develop a living practice to switch off all electronic devices and remove oneself from the daily feeds of social platform news and updates.

The more One removes the 'white noise' of society and the pulse of egoic images, thought streams and negative energy, the better One's life will be. Turn off to tune in to One's inner spiritual landscape of peace, harmony, balance, love, contentment and inner joy in this world. One already has direct access to One's spirit and the universe now. One simply needs to be present in the moment.

> *Realize deeply that the present moment is all you have.*
> *Make the NOW the primary focus of your life.*
> Eckhart Tolle

Be mindful about living life now. One does this by staying focused on living with purposeful intent. If One is drinking tea, drink as if it is the last tea that One will ever have. Train One's mind and body to enjoy whatever One is engaged in now without the expectation that it must deliver something other than what it is.

Be accepting and giving to all

Accept where One is now. Wherever One is in this world at this moment in time is where One needs to begin. Even in a world currently and predominantly driven by egoic laws, structures, systems, institutions, companies and relationships, One does not need to be like everyone else on the planet.

One can accept things as they are, but One does not need to be complicit with them. People are responsible for One's own actions in life. One also has a choice to live life from a higher level of consciousness through being a better version of oneself.

> *Be a gift to everyone who enters your life, and to everyone whose life you enter. Be careful not to enter another's life if you cannot be a gift.*
> Neale Donald Walsch

When One takes personal responsibility for One's own life, thoughts, feelings, emotions, behaviours, habits and actions. One is on the right path to experiencing a higher vibration of existence in this world. The way that One changes the people and world around One is first by changing oneself. One does this by accepting all of oneself first. This includes One's flaws, faults and faux pas.

Observe oneself and others in a loving, caring, kind and compassionate way. Do not criticise; encourage all to cultivate a spirit-centric view of oneself, others and the world. Give oneself and others space and time to be who One chooses to be now. Without judgement, gently suggest and enthusiastically encourage all along a better path to a more rewarding, purposeful and meaningful outcome in life. Just because pain, suffering and trauma exist in people's lives does not mean that it has to continue forever. One can give oneself the gift of freedom from these experiences. One does this by accepting that One needs to positively change now. As One changes, One enables a different perspective, belief, sense of living wellness and coherence (mind–body–spirit) within oneself.

Inner change and spiritual alignment are gifts to a brighter and better future for all.

Trust the process

Sometimes the wrong way is the right path for people who are still trying to figure out how to transform oneself (mind–body–spirit), One's life and One's way in the world.

As challenging as it is, One has to trust One's spirit, trust the process and trust 'the way' of the universe. Do not be too concerned about arriving at One's desired outcome or divine destiny. Simply focus on the process in front of One now and let the universe take care of the rest, as it has always done.

Finding One's way in life can sometimes be fraught with personal challenges, misleading information and unhelpful ego-centric people. One will need to navigate all these obstacles along One's journey and find an inner way to where One needs to be now. Like a flower waiting for the sun to rise before it opens, be patient and solutions will come to One at the right moment. In the meantime, focus on living life with a sense of positive optimism that everything will work out for One. Imbue One's outlook in the world with the intention that all the answers will be revealed to One when this needs to happen. Stay open, be aware and let oneself flow with the natural rhythm of the day and night. In addition, be mindful and reflective of One's life on the planet. Be grateful each day that One is alive and give thanks for the blessings before One. Stay fluid, flexible, adaptable and spiritually centred now.

Look at your mind dispassionately; this is enough to calm it. When it is quiet, you can go beyond it. Do not keep it busy all the time. Stop it – just be. If you give it rest, it will settle down and recover its purity and strength. Constant thinking makes it decay.
Nisargadatta Maharaj

The Moon does not question its orbit around the Earth and the Earth does not question its orbit around the Sun. Both are freely in motion without judgement, attachment or resisting this changing lifecycle. The Moon trusts the Earth, the Earth trusts the Sun and the Sun trusts the universe to hold it securely, safely and within the sanctuary of its celestial embrace. One should do the same – let go and trust the universe to honour One's spirit, higher self and infinite existence in the cosmos.

One's path in life may not always be clear. This is okay. It gives One a chance to pause, be still and momentarily reflect on where One is now. Know that the universe did not magically all come into existence in a single moment. Everything that ever was or will ever be evolved out of something else. This is the same for One's life on Earth too.

If things are not working in One's life then choose to change 'the way' One's life is working. Be grateful for all the good things, playful pleasures and memorable moments that One has had the opportunity to experience – the air that One breathes, the food that One eats, the water that One drinks, the sleep that One enjoys, the people in One's life, the love that One has shared, and the land beneath One's feet, the lakes, rivers and seas that cover the Earth and the sky above One.

> **Within the 'NOW' of this moment, everyone and everything exists.**

One cannot go above it, beneath it, behind it or in front of it. But when the mind is still, calm and silent, One is able to go beyond it. It is in this space of peaceful tranquillity that One can align with One's spirit, soul or cosmic consciousness. What One will find here is the spiritual sanctuary that One has been seeking throughout One's entire life. This inner way is a path to freedom from the constant pressures, stress, anxiety, depression, negative thoughts and self-limiting beliefs in contemporary society. Modern life has a way of negatively impacting upon all the human senses – sight, sound, touch, taste and smell.

One of the best ways to shield oneself from this disabling and destructive energy is to live a spirit-centric life. Coupled with this approach, One also needs to create a mindful living presence in everything that One thinks, says and does in the community or world.

A simple strategy to avoid being sucked into the vortex of negative and toxic energy of other people is learning to operate at a higher level of consciousness. This will naturally protect oneself from people who are choosing to operate at a lower level of consciousness in the community and society at large.

As One chooses to live life from this spiritual perspective, it will bring greater clarity to oneself, One's life and One's way in the world.

Do not underestimate One's power to change the way that One thinks, lives, works and plays. As One changes oneself to be more 'in tune' with One's inner spirit, soul or cosmic consciousness, One also realigns One's entire life to a new trajectory on the planet. The spiritual arc of One's life can and will be altered when One makes a conscious decision to exist as a sentient Being of the universe on Earth now. When One does this, it will have a very dramatic effect on One's life. It usually means that One will need to leave some people behind. This is not because these individuals are unworthy, it is because One's vibrating resonant energy is at a level that is out of sync with these people.

One will find oneself being drawn to a different path in life. A path that is focused on being spiritually centred, prosperous, abundant and fully awake now. The things that use to distract One's attention and waste One's time previously will have no appeal. This will naturally encourage One to be more mindful, not just about how One uses One's time, but where One invests One's energy throughout the day and with whom. This is all part of trusting the path before One as it reveals itself in the moment.

Although the outcome for life on the planet for everyone is the same, each person must discover One's own path forward along 'the way' of this spiritual journey of inner enlightenment, self-realisation and divine awakening. No two people are the same and no two paths are exactly alike. What will work for one person may not necessarily work for another. Each individual must walk One's own path and be the light in the darkness for One to see 'the way'. To know the path, One must become the path. There are no shortcuts to the process other than preparing One's passage so that it aligns with One's spirit and the universe now.

Keep moving forward – remember and memorise this.

> One is the creator of One's reality, life and future on Earth.

Just do what needs to be done

The idea of humankind spiritually evolving and transforming Earth into an interstellar Type 1 civilisation in the near future may seem far-fetched, but it is a goal that everyone can strive towards if we work in partnership and harmony with each other. This can be achieved if One makes small changes in One's daily life. By doing so, individuals can not only help to create a better future for oneself, but also contribute to the betterment of humanity as a whole. Here are just six of the many key benefits that taking simple actions now to create great changes on the planet can bring.

Spiritual consciousness

By aligning with One's spirit, soul or consciousness, One can improve the coherence of One's mind–body–spirit in One's daily life. This will reduce stress and improve One's divine connection within and with other sentient Beings in the world as well as other living entities in this galaxy. One's overall life will be significantly enhanced as One becomes more spiritually aware and awake. This will naturally lead to a rise in the level of collective consciousness and vibration of all living Beings on the Earth.

Natural and social justice

Supporting and voting to return stolen and/or occupied Country (land, sea and sky) and making adequate restitution and/or compensation to First Nations is a great first step in creating peace, prosperity and abundance for all. This can be achieved through changes to the constitution and laws of nation-states so that they align with natural and social justice principles and establish a fair, reasonable and equitable life trajectory for all First Nations' people. This will ensure access to and management of First Nations' natural resources on Country around the planet. The flow-on effects will further improve and increase the incidents of whole-of-life wellness, individual and collective wellbeing, wellships, sociocultural connection within First Nations' families and communities now and for future generations. It will set the scene for a more mature partnership and mutually beneficial relationship moving forward on the Earth.

Eco-friendly sustainability

By reducing One's carbon footprint and adopting more sustainable practices, One can help to create a more stable and resilient planet for future generations. This includes reducing energy consumption through the efficient use of renewable energy sources, reducing waste through recycling and composting, and reducing and eventually removing the use of single-use plastics.

Improved quality of life

By reducing pollution and preserving natural resources, One can improve the health and wellbeing of all living Beings on the planet. This will lead to better air quality, cleaner water sources and healthier food options, resulting in improved physical, mental and spiritual health, wellships with others and wellbeing for everyone.

Economic stability

By investing in stable, circular financial systems that promote sustainable technologies and practices to lower the cost of living, One can create alternative independent economic 'fair trade' systems and zones that ensure pathways of prosperity for individuals, families and communities. This will see the creation of 'real world' new jobs in industries such as renewable energy, AI and digital computing, recycling, personal support, mentoring, coaching, professional wellness therapies and sustainable 'clean-green' mini-macro place-based agriculture. The benefits will include – but not be limited to – boosting local economies, increasing wellness, promoting intelligent living and reducing poverty and inequality. It will also promote prosperity and abundance on the planet.

Space exploration

By advancing space technology, interstellar information and interplanetary infrastructure, One can make space exploration and tourism a reality. This can bring numerous benefits to humanity, such as the discovery of new resources, the development of new technologies, exploration of space, living on other planets and the expansion of human knowledge as well as contact with friendly extra-terrestrial entities or sentient Beings.

Enabling a new future on Earth now

Consciously minded and awakened humans need to get on with the job of enabling a new future on Earth now. One is capable of significantly and radically improving oneself and the lives of others on Earth. By rising above One's current circumstances, personal issues or individual fears, One can become aware of One's inner spirit and One's divine connection with the universe. In addition, One can create great positive change in One's life on the planet. One will be able to simplify complex systems and align with the new age of enlightenment or awakened thoughts, vibrations and changes in the world. With every new day, One can be creative about One's life and let go of One's past lapses in judgement and egoic choices. By following simple steps, such as releasing, removing and refocusing, One can let go of lingering thoughts and feelings of remorse and embarrassment. This will enable One to recreate One's new life with the support of friends, family and others such as lifestyle coaches, living mentors, wellness professionals and the universe.

Do not be tempted to stay in the perspective of only 'being human' because it is safe, secure and comforting. Just because it is the only thing that One has ever known or believed since coming to Earth does not mean that One needs to be trapped by this inherited intergenerational hand-me-down thought of oneself in the world today. Embrace the living duality of the world and then rise above it by choosing to be a 'Bright' – an awakened sentient Being of the universe now.

Take the initiative to improve oneself and the lives of others on the planet. Do not procrastinate or waste One's life energy, space or time on Earth. It is time to influence the world and nudge people's consciousness into a higher level of inner awareness.

The stepping stones to the future already exist within One's Being. Like a helium balloon floating freely in the sky, keep rising to greater and greater heights of self-awareness and inner reflection. As One lets go of the past, One can see with increased clarity the world in which One was raised and how to rise above it.

Learn to move beyond the pettiness of humanity's ego-centric ways of living in denial about One's spirit, soul or cosmic consciousness. Become aware of the social systems of control and containment to keep One a prisoner in financial debt and a captive of economic slavery. Discover how to free oneself of One's ego and then do what must be done to create change in One's life so that One is true to One's inner spirit and flowing with 'the way' of the universe.

Many may see this challenge as overwhelming or too difficult a concept to accept. Rest assured, the solution to what must be done is as easy as breathing now. The dismantling of any complex living or artificial system is to first see it as 'simplicity in chaos'. Everything can be simplified into its component parts, just like Lego bricks, and put back together again using the same pieces, but with a different intention, and in a way that aligns with a new way of thinking, perceiving and manifesting One's new reality.

Self-organising theory suggests that components or elements within systems naturally align in vibrational harmony with one another, meaning that, as One begins to change, things, people, places and processes around One will naturally align to these new thoughts, vibrations and changes too. The longer One stays in the vibration, the greater the alignment of One's world will appear to magically sync with this vision, perception or imagined reality. Hence, if One can believe it, think it, imagine it, feel it – it is highly likely that One will realise it, manifest it and experience it now.

This is why One's new world will come into being with the support of others with similar intentions and in alignment with a new vision to co-create an alternative reality on this planet – an interstellar spiritually united Type 1 civilisation on Earth. Know that the universe is on One's side too.

> Little by little, step by step and moment by moment the world is created into what One imagines it to be now.

Letting go

Even though there are only 24 hours in a day, a lot can be done in this time. With every new day, One has a new opportunity to be creative about One's life and how One chooses to live it. Do not continually punish oneself for One's past decisions, poor judgements or accidental mistakes that One may have made while in different jobs, relationships or investments. Do not dwell on what One may have said to a friend or how One behaved with others at the time. Learn to let go and forgive oneself now and forever. It is time to move forward. Release oneself of all the guilt, shame, expectations, thoughts and energies that One has accumulated over time. Empty oneself completely and embrace the unknown emptiness and inner space. Know that One is spirit, not this mental construct within One's mind – it does not belong here now or in the future. One is free to recreate and reimagine One's new life and reality on Earth now.

There are three simple steps to assist One to let go:
- release
- remove
- refocus.

Release

Release One's inner thoughts and energy within oneself and towards others unconditionally and completely without any reservations. Know that everything in life can be used to assist One to align with One's higher self and help One awaken. Releasing or forgiving is not about giving up, ceasing to make an effort or admitting defeat. It is simply about surrendering to the 'now' in life and shifting One's present coherent (mind–body–spirit) energy. To release and forgive is an act of compassion towards oneself and a way to transform any issues, concerns or worries and energies into a higher vibrational state that One may have in regard to another person's ideas, attitudes, personhood, behaviours, actions or energies in this life.

Release affirmation

One compassionately and unconditionally releases oneself and others of any and all negative, hurtful or egoic actions implied or otherwise directed at oneself. One lets go of any and all toxic emotions, harmful judgements and dark energy within One's mind–body and unlocks a doorway to inner peace, harmony and joy in One's life now. One chooses to be free at this moment and every moment from now on as long as One lives. One consciously and willingly decides to embrace love, unity and oneness within the coherence of One's mind–body–spirit and express it in every aspect of One's life on Earth, today – tomorrow – forevermore.

Remove

Remove oneself from One's egoic intentions, behaviours, habits and actions of the past. What has happened has already happened and nothing One can do can change anything that has happened in One's life. Whatever feelings and thoughts One has about this activity, situation or event – simply acknowledge it for what it was, when it was, how it was and then let it go and dissolve it into the nothingness of eternal existence. Life is meant to be lived in the present now. Learn from it to guide One's new direction in life so One can become the best version of oneself at this moment.

Refocus

Find a way to positively move forward by creating a new reality and manifesting this new future here on Earth today. Be open to everything and attached to nothing as One purposely changes and deliberately discovers a new direction in life. As One focuses One's energy on creating these new experiences in the world, One will also be creating new pathways and networks in the brain that align with this new reality on the planet. The more One focuses One's energy on this new space, the faster and stronger the wiring will be in One's brain that supports this new thinking and feelings. Hence, imagine only the best outcome for oneself and live it now. Live with purpose as a Being of light, love and oneness and so it will be.

Simple actions

For an average person, taking simple actions to create great changes on the planet is a very real option. Here are some suggestions.

Spiritual consciousness

Believing in One's spirit, soul or cosmic consciousness and aligning in coherence mind–body–spirit on a daily basis through mindfulness and meditation practices. Having deep and meaningful conversations with others about the need to change and become less ego centred and live a more of a spirit-centric way of life on the planet.

Natural and social justice

Talking about, working in partnerships with others, advocating for and voting for change by casting One's votes to support legislation, laws, and on-the-ground policies and practices to address social justice issues for First Nations' people and other issues in the community.

Conserving energy

Turning off lights and unplugging electronic devices when not in use, using energy-efficient appliances and light bulbs, and carpooling or using public transportation.

Reducing waste

Recycling and composting, reducing the use of single-use plastics, and supporting companies that use sustainable packaging. Supporting a 'zero-waste' culture and economy in society from concept to consumer. Choosing only products that have an energy-efficient post-production or manufacturing deconstruction process or are biodegradable.

> **Supporting sustainable agriculture**
>
> Choosing to eat locally sourced, organic, and plant-based foods, and supporting sustainable 'paddock to plate' farming practices.

> **Investing in renewable and interstellar energy technologies**
>
> Supporting local action in the community and with social enterprise companies that use renewable energy sources, investing in renewable and interstellar energy technology, and advocating for government policies that promote true sustainable energy or 'no-cost' placed-based practices.

These actions may seem small and insignificant, but when taken by millions of people, One can have a profound impact on the planet and help to achieve the goal of becoming an interstellar spiritually united Type 1 civilisation in the near future.

IMPORTANT LEARNINGS, TEACHINGS AND POINTINGS

Key ways to live life as spirit, soul or cosmic consciousness

 If One seeks a new life in this world, One will need to imagine a new vision for oneself. What One believes – One imagines. What One imagines – One creates within One's mind and then can manifest it in the 'real world'.

 Where One's focus goes, One's energy flows. The first step in accessing One's infinite potential is knowing of its existence within oneself now. Know that One is an indomitable spirit with powers beyond measure in this world. One is special, unique and an integral part of the universe.

 The seven keys to personal empowerment and transformation are:

Key 1: Awaken to spirit, soul or cosmic consciousness within oneself

Key 2: Believe in oneself as a sentient Being of the universe

Key 3: Create a clear new vision of the future

Key 4: Act with proactive intent, genuine honesty and spiritual integrity

Key 5: Be present in every living moment in life

Key 6: Flow in coherence, cooperation and co-existence with all

Key 7: Live life as a spiritual and mindful practice now

 Everything that One aspires to in life is possible with a loving spirit, kind heart, an open mind and a vision of the future where One is free of egoic fears and false truths in this world.

- Be spiritually in sync
- Adapt, evolve and innovate
- Be realistic, relevant and reflective
- Continually improve oneself (mind-body-spirit)
- Be aware and open to everything
- Listen, learn and live life now
- Be accepting and giving to all

 To truly transform oneself (mind-body-spirit), One's life and One's way in the world simply trust One's spirit and the universe. Keep moving forward - One is the creator of One's reality, life and future on Earth.

 There are three simple steps or strategies to assist One to let go:

Step 1: Release - oneself and others unconditionally today.

Step 2: Remove - past issues, concerns and worries at this moment.

Step 3: Refocus - on the present and create a new future reality now.

PART FIVE

Transcend to an awakened consciousness

One's spiritual purpose on this planet

Discovering One's spiritual purpose on Earth is an important aspect of human life. It can help individuals find meaning, direction and living contentment. It can also play a crucial role in assisting humanity to evolve on the planet by promoting individual and collective inner growth, creating a more compassionate and harmonious society, and establishing a prosperous and abundant world. There are many reasons why discovering One's spiritual purpose is important for both the individual and humanity as a whole.

Undergo change and personal growth

When individuals understand One's spiritual purpose, One is able to make decisions that align with One's values, virtues and beliefs. This can lead to greater inner peace, happiness, and contentment, as well as improved personal relationships, partnerships and a greater sense of connectedness with others.

Improved mental wellbeing

Engaging in activities that align with One's spiritual purpose can have a positive impact on One's mental wellbeing and wellship with others in One's life. Research has shown that spirituality can provide comfort, support and a sense of hope during difficult times, which can reduce stress and anxiety. It can also improve One's resilience, coping strategies and inspire a positive outlook for the future.

Increased self-awareness and compassion

When individuals understand One's spiritual purpose, One is more likely to be self-aware, compassionate and empathetic towards others. This can lead to greater understanding and acceptance of different cultures, religions and beliefs, promoting a more harmonious and peaceful world.

Sense of spiritual oneness or community

By connecting with others who share similar spiritual beliefs, individuals can form strong bonds, deep connections and a sense of oneness or spiritual community. This can provide a supportive network and a sense of belonging, which is important for the overall wellbeing of a person and the collective wellness of the family and community wellship in which One lives.

Better understanding of One's place in the world

Discovering One's spiritual purpose can provide a greater understanding of One's place in the world and the role One plays in the larger picture of life on the planet. This can lead to a greater appreciation for the world around One and a desire to make a positive impact on all future generations in the world.

Does it feel sometimes like One's life doesn't have a purpose? Does One find oneself thinking that One's job is pointless? That anyone could do it, or that no one would notice if it wasn't done at all? Does One's relationships feel empty and alone? Does it feel that if One just dropped off the face of the Earth, scarcely anyone would notice? There's no reason to feel ashamed of feeling this way. Many people do on the planet.

But One shouldn't feel this way – right? Because One does have a purpose, One just hasn't discovered it yet until now.

One's divine purpose on this planet is to be consciously awake now. Then live life in joyful bliss as an expression of One's cosmic divinity through One's human form. When One understands this completely – to the depth of One's spirit, soul and cosmic consciousness – it will change the very fabric of the quantum unified field of conscious reality that exists within One's Being forever.

Coming to terms with this changes everything and everything is changed with this 'divine knowing'. One's ego may try and resist this thought, idea or concept but this struggle will fail in the end. The more One tries to force meaning into One's life, the more One will appreciate that meaning is derived from One's purpose here on Earth. One's purpose is simple: 'Be awake now'. What comes next will be revealed to One along 'the way'. Just be present wherever One is now.

One could do ten thousand things in this world and be the best at every single one of them. But if One is not awake, One is simply living in a dream world of One's own egoic making. One is just going through the motions of life, living day by day with no awareness of who One truly is as a sentient Being of the universe. One is not the driver of One's life, One is driven by One's subconscious egoic social conditioning and cultural programming. Ever since One was a child in this world, One has had the potential to be awake and live a spiritually centric life.

For most people living in the world today. One's experiences have been moulded, managed and manipulated in such a way as to distort, distract and disregard One's inner spirit or divine Being. Years of social conditioning and cultural programming in schools, families, communities, society, First Nations and nation-states have reinforced the idea that spirit, soul or cosmic consciousness does not exist and is not to be validated in any way. It is essentially written out of the contemporary landscape of current conversations in favour of relentless commercialism and capitalist motives of prioritising profits over people on the planet.

However, as each generation becomes more and more aware of who One truly is as spirit, it is beginning to change the living landscape on Earth. This shift is creating an ever-increasing interest in looking towards a new event horizon that reshapes, reconfigures and reframes the world from a more spiritually centred perspective. A world view is emerging that is starting to influence social conversations on various media platforms that speak to living and being in the world from an alternative point of view. Slowly but surely, more and more people on the planet are waking up and raising One's level of consciousness. This act of individual self-realisation will eventually come to a shared event of 'global awakening'.

Today is the beginning of the best days of One's life on Earth. From now on, embrace the thought, feeling and vibration that only good comes to One. While 'good' may be an emotional and subjective term, it is a reasonable observation that One can make about One's life at this moment. Welcome, invite and imagine only good things, good people, good opportunities, good experiences, good relationships, good health and good times. Simply focus on believing it – affirming it – expressing it – manifesting it – receiving it now. As the purpose of One's life is revealed to One, it will all make sense. Let everything come to One in its own way. Do not chase after fame, fortune or an egoic future. What will come, will arrive when it does. What will not, wasn't meant for One anyway. So be it now.

Allow the abundance of the universe to flow through One at this moment. Do not waste One's time and life needlessly wishing and wanting for things, people or experiences to improve One's life in this world. Wanting stuff or material things from an egoic perspective only reinforces a state of lacking in One's life. Instead, live life from a higher vibration and see oneself in a state of realised abundance and gratitude. Be grateful for all the good things, people and experiences in One's life. Look not to sell but to share things and experiences with others.

Know that freedom only comes when One is free. This may seem very obvious, but many people in the world are still trying to be free through more and more attachment to things. These people think if only One can obtain a certain level of income or accumulate money, assets and status to a certain value then One will be free. Sadly, this is a false promise and a misleading daydream. Yes, on the surface it has worked for some, but in most cases for most people in the world, it has not. One needs to understand that the capitalist system of the Western world has been engineered from an egoic perspective based on a disempowering framework. This human artificial construct is about keeping people in economic slavery from one generation to the next. The outcome of this socioeconomic cultural algorithm is to promote a process that keeps most of the population in perpetual poverty and attached to a perception of ongoing powerlessness in the world.

> *We have deluded ourselves into believing the myth that capitalism grew and prospered out of the Protestant ethic of hard work and sacrifice. The fact is that capitalism was built on the exploitation and suffering of black slaves and continues to thrive on the exploitation of the poor – both black and white, here and abroad.*
> Martin Luther King Jr

The ongoing subtle and sublime messaging of this egoic capitalist system is that if One works hard enough, long enough and is smart enough, One will be able to accumulate enough money to set oneself up and be free. Unfortunately, most people believe this false doctrine or fake narrative. It is like a casino where the odds are stacked in the house's favour the more One plays the game. The odds are statistically engineered in favour of maintaining and feeding this egoic capitalist system the more One participates in it.

Being free begins by being consciously aware and spiritually awake now. When One is awake, One can rise above the ordinary and become something truly special in this world. Do not wait for another day or another person to come along to free oneself. One must take responsibility for the changes that One must make in One's life today.

It is no surprise that the more wisdom that One attains and the more consciously aware One becomes, the crazier One will appear to others in the world. Know this truth and be prepared to stand up, step forward and stay true to One's inner spirit and divine Being. Keep believing in One's spirit, oneself (mind–body–spirit) and One's way on the planet. Know that something very good is coming One's way. Good news – great times and many wonderful blessings.

Prepare One's life to be purposeful each day that One is on Earth now. Find a quiet place in the morning and be still so One can align with One's spirit, soul or cosmic consciousness. When in this relaxed mind–body–spirit state, slowly expand One's inner awareness out from One's heart into the world and universe. Intentionally envision all the good things, thoughts, feelings and experiences that will come effortlessly into One's life. Allow oneself to feel all the amazing qualities that resonate with this imaginary new life and reality on Earth as if it is already here today. Open One's heart, soul or spirit to these new and wonderful emotions (thoughts and feelings) now. Be in a state of infinite gratitude for any and all gifts, as if they are present now in One's life.

Make this purposeful practice a mindful meditation habit. Organise it as part of One's daily routine and spiritual lifestyle in the community. As One aligns more closely to One's purpose One will become more in sync with the natural rhythm and harmony of the universe. Things will seamlessly flow forward along One's spiritual purpose in life. Simply let go and allow oneself to journey along this path of prosperity, abundance and wakefulness.

Being present on Earth at this moment

Being present on Earth at this moment is incredibly significant for several reasons. This is a time in human history where we have unprecedented opportunities for progress and positive change, but also face significant challenges that require One's attention and action. There are many reasons why being present on Earth at this moment matters so much to individuals and the survival of humanity. These include, but are not limited to, the following:

- Spiritual unity and enabling the collective consciousness of everyone on the planet to come together in harmony and changing the trajectory of all life so that it creates a new reality in the world – an interstellar spiritually united Type 1 civilisation on Earth.
- Climate change and taking action to address the rising temperature and sea levels on the planet.
- Social justice and working to create a more just and equitable world, where everyone has the opportunity to thrive, regardless of their race, gender, location or socioeconomic status.
- Technological progress to contribute to reduced living costs, improve quality of life and help shape the future of 'human friendly' technology in a way that benefits everyone.
- Health and wellbeing to have access to better healthcare, better nutrition and better mental health information, advice, referral, support and resources that inspire and create a healthier, happier, and more a prosperous, abundant and contented life.

Being present on Earth at this moment is incredibly important because it gives One the opportunity to make a positive impact on the world and shape the future in a way that benefits everyone. While there are many challenges facing people everywhere on the planet, there are also many opportunities for progress and positive change. By being present and engaged in the world around One, One can help to create a brighter future for oneself and new generations.

Being present on Earth as a spiritual sentient Being at this moment is of utmost importance. The world is rapidly changing and it is critical to be present in One's life to make the most of it each and every day that One is alive. When One is present, One does not need to impose One's will or control over anything in life – One simply needs to remain still and centred.

The world is changing fast, and it is essential to adapt and grow with the changing times. One must be patient, trust the process, believe in One's spirit and look for the signs of change along 'the way' to a brighter future. Most importantly, One must live in the present moment and walk slowly, savouring each step, bringing One to the best moment of one's life.

When One is truly present, One does not need to force anything to happen in life. All One needs to do is surrender, have faith and observe as everything unfolds perfectly for One.

Anything that you fully accept will take you into peace. This is the miracle of surrender.
Eckhart Tolle

Know that One is on the right planet, amongst the right people, with the right purpose, to do the right things and enable the right future for everyone on Earth. A future reality where everyone everywhere is living a life aligned to One's divine purpose within an interstellar spiritually united Type 1 civilisation on Earth now.

Be grateful that One is here on this planet doing what needs to be done to create positive change in One's life and the world. Investing in One's mind–body–spirit to be a better version of oneself is key to making this happen today. Know that there are no coincidences in the universe. The future is coming to One today. Everything that One has asked the universe for during this life is already on its way to One. One simply needs to be patient, pay attention to the signs, flow with life and enable the right conditions for these experiences and a new reality to manifest itself now.

If you want to succeed in life, remember this phrase. The past does not equal the future. Because you failed yesterday; or all day today, or a moment ago, or the last six months; the last sixteen years, or the last fifty years of life doesn't mean anything ... all that matters is what are you going to do, right now?
Anthony Robins

Learn to keep One's energy high, trust the process, believe in One's spirit, and look for and see the signs of change along 'the way' to a brighter future. Radiate One's positivity, love, optimism, faith, gentleness, care, kindness and compassion out into the world and universe each and every day that One is alive. Teach and train One's mind–body to turn One's 'should do's' into 'must do's' through intentional action today.

So live your life that the fear of death can never enter your heart ... Love your life, perfect your life, beautify all things in your life. Seek to make your life long and its purpose in the service of your people.
Tecumseh

Do not look backwards at the failures or mistakes in One's life and ask 'Why me?' Instead, look forward towards a fantastic future or amazing reality and ask 'Why not?' Believe that One is worthy of great experiences and good times. A life that is free from fear, debt and attachment to negative low-energy habits, behaviours, emotions (thoughts and feelings) as well as material objects and people. Imagine and look forward to living a life overflowing with grace, gratitude and generosity.

Even if One's path does not seem clear at this time, stay present within oneself and simply wait for the fog and uncertainty to clear in One's mind. Give oneself space, time and an opportunity to simply breathe or take a break. Look after oneself through mindful meditation practices and allow One's mind to release any and all attached thoughts. Be aware of what One is carrying around in One's mind and One's self-talk throughout the day.

> **Everything changes in life and life changes everything.**

Learn how to flip the script of any negative internal chatter like 'I can't', 'I am not worthy', 'I will most likely fail' to positive messages such as 'One has got this', 'One is worthy and deserves love, attention and affection' and 'One will be successful no matter what happens in life'. Given enough practice, this will become an automatic response within One's thought process. It will also set up a new neural pathway that will change the internal wiring of One's brain and create a new positive network of connections.

Reality is created by the mind. We can change our reality by changing our mind.
Plato

One has the indomitable power to create any reality that One dares to imagine now. The question One needs to ask oneself is: Does One have the will, courage and commitment to make these changes to oneself (mind–body–spirit) and One's life?

To mindfully and consciously give the best of oneself to others, One must first give to oneself. This is not about being selfish, it is all about being sensible, practical and reasonable. Fill One's own well of wellness from the eternal spring of life so that others may drink from it if need be. Always take time to constantly replenish One's own mind–body energy with plenty of rest, adequate sleep, nutritious food, gentle exercise and positive social contact in the community. Establish a daily routine that supports One's alignment with spirit and meditation practices that promote mind–body–spirit coherence. Review the section 'Developing One's spiritual toolbox for life' in Part 4 for hints and tips on how One can invest in creating a more harmonious, balanced and positive spirit-centric lifestyle.

Walk slow. Don't rush. Each step brings you to the best moment of your life, the present moment.
Thich Nhat Hanh

In broad terms, most modern-day non-believers or spiritual doubters will move through a three-stage spiritual discovery process. First, people will refute and deny that spirit, soul or cosmic consciousness is true. Second, people will reject and disagree that it is important or relevant to One's life on Earth. Finally, people who have self-realised and become 'awake' will embrace One's cosmic consciousness or celestial divinity within oneself as a sentient Being or spirit of the universe.

The future will look very different moving forward from this point on for 'awake' individuals. These people will consciously choose **not** to focus on accumulating material objects, hoarding money or engaging in relationships with other people for pure personal gain. Awake people's perspective will have dramatically shifted to view the world through an altered lens in this present moment. One will be inclined to see the positive potential of changing the very fabric of space–time that One is living in at this moment. In addition, awake people will view all living situations and circumstances through a filter of the dynamic duality of choice. They will also tend to observe everything as existing in the now or quantum consciousness unified field. This mindful and spiritual presence will influence the energy and matter that One exists in now. It will also influence those individuals that One meets daily and throughout One's life on the planet.

Being mindfully and spiritually present is not about staying still in life or doing nothing about changing One's personal circumstances or continuing to do whatever One is doing today in a quiet way. It is about realising that One is intrinsically linked to, part of and exists within the conscious sea of everything now.

Being present in the world is a natural state of One's divine Being or consciousness. It is one of the seven states of consciousness that already exist within One. One does not need to strive for it, One simply needs to align with One's inner spirit, soul or cosmic consciousness now.

> One's spiritual presence is extremely powerful. It has the potential to create incredible, inspiring and amazing changes within oneself and influence others on Earth.

Being present in another person's life is a powerful tool for personal growth, individual development, transformative change and spiritual enlightenment. The energetic energy field that One can bring to any situation simply by being present at the moment can shift the energy of another person or an entire room, group or gathering of people. Do not underestimate the 'power of presence' to influence, shift and shape the present reality of One's life and the lives of others in this world.

Choosing the right path, process and practice to awaken now

There is only 'the way' to where One needs to be now. Each person's path on the planet will look and feel different along One's individual journey in life. However, the outcome is the same. Everyone returns to Source someday – today, tomorrow or in the future. One thing is certain is that everyone's human form on Earth will eventually die and One's molecules will disassemble back into the stardust from which it originated. It is then that a new adventure begins in the universe. So, in the meantime, do not rush life. Let it flow within One today. Allow oneself to simply be fully present in the moment now.

Many people currently on the planet are searching or seeking answers to life and life's challenges through external means. These people are hoping to find answers outside oneself or in another person.

While in some individual circumstances, people do come across gems of information, inspiration and wisdom, for the most part, people seem to aimlessly stumble through life in an unawakened state.

Most paths in life appear to lead somewhere else in the world other than being where One is now. Some people may ask: 'What is the right path in life?' In response to this question, there is no single answer that will satisfy One's egoic mind. One needs to get comfortable with uncertainty in this life. A cloud does not have any concerns about which way the wind is blowing, it just flows effortlessly along and in the direction of the current at the time. One should see One's path like a freshwater stream flowing to a river and then that river flowing to the ocean. When One lets go of looking for the path, the path will present itself to One. This is how it works – naturally and effortlessly in sync with the rhythm of the universe.

Do not try to find it – simply flow with it now. This is 'the way' to become what One needs to be at this moment.

Know that to get to where One needs to be, One will have to ask the right question. Do not ask: 'How does One get there?' Instead, ask: 'How does One live a life that is in coherence with mind–body–spirit and aligns with the synchronicity of the universe?'

Asking a different question about oneself and the universe will often give One a different response and direction in life. Sometimes this new answer may be something that One has not thought of before or was simply too blind to see in the moment. Breaking the cycle of ingrained behaviours, repetitive thoughts and familiar life patterns of the past requires One to become self-aware of One's current social and cultural egoic programming. Just because One has thought and done things to get where One is today does not mean that One needs to continue thinking and doing those same things tomorrow. Life is about living with change and changing with life.

To evolve as a spiritual Being in this life, One must learn to continually shed One's 'human skin' of personality or egoic persona like a snake, or become a grub that metamorphoses into a beautiful butterfly again and again throughout One's lifetime.

Give oneself space to change, time to evolve and the opportunity to be the best version of oneself on this planet. Even if One cannot see it now, One's path and direction in life require care, kindness and compassion on a daily basis.

Pay no particular attention to what others may say or how these people may react to One's new spirit-centric view and attitude towards oneself. A lesser egoic mind will always react out of fear and from a lower vibration or with a self-absorbed attitude of 'What is in it for me?'

> *People have a hard time of letting go of their suffering. Out of a fear of the unknown, they prefer suffering that is familiar.*
> Thich Nhat Hanh

It is time to inspire and encourage oneself along One's true divine path in life. Do not think about what may or may not happen in a week, a month or even a year. Just stay in the moment and focus on One's stress-free and seamless passage through the next twenty-four hours. Only do what can be done in this present moment and intentionally take action to complete One's life priorities today. With every breath that One takes and every step that One makes, One is moving in a positive direction to where One needs to be now.

One's spiritual journey will always be more important than One's human destination in this world.

Some people may think that if only One can see the future, One would be able to avoid all the potential mistakes One may make in life. This preventative thinking is good if One wishes to do no self-harm. However, it is important to know that growth and personal development cannot take place in the absence of change and change often requires One to experience personal pain. Therefore, the journey is part of the process and One simply needs to trust the process.

One is not behind where One needs to be in life, nor is One too late to take action to improve One's spiritual connection or change One's life trajectory. One is exactly where One is meant to be now. Do not be hard on oneself if One is still yet to see certain results, outputs or outcomes – all things change in life and life changes all things.

Everything passes – rivers flow, the Moon glows and the stars come and go in the night sky.

Wishing or wanting a perfect life story, marriage, partnership, lover, family, life experience or ending is not how the universe works. One needs to learn that some things just fall apart no matter how much energy and positivity One puts into the situation or relationship. On the other hand, sometimes things come together effortlessly, as if by magic, with little or minimal positive energy or commitment. The universe has a way of working everything out in the best interests of One's higher self. This is why it is so important to reflect on One's positive spiritual intent in life and live in gratitude for everything that the universe has to offer One too. Acceptance is the key to living an awakened life where One is present in every moment of One's life on Earth.

One's inner ego will always cloud and confuse One's mind in an effort to hide One's true path. One's egoic ways will stop with every individual person on the planet making a conscious decision to stop it now. This will give rise to the beginning of One's new spirit-centric ways with every person too. When One dives deep enough into One's spirit, soul or cosmic consciousness, One will find a new beginning and be able to start again. Nothing is so complicated, messed up or broken within oneself that One cannot begin again in this world. Anything can be healed with love, kindness, care and compassion. One need only create the space and give oneself the time to journey into self-healing to restore, refresh and renew One's emotional, mental, physical and spiritual wellbeing. Inner wellness comes from being well within One's mind–body–spirit and having positive wellships with others.

To give openly, honestly and genuinely to oneself is an act of spiritual awakening and part of One's spiritual evolution on Earth.

One person alone cannot bear the responsibility for or change the world to make it a better place for all future generations. It will take everyone everywhere making individual changes on a daily basis. However, One can take radical responsibility to transform One's own level of consciousness so that it operates at a higher frequency in alignment with One's higher spiritual self. This can be achieved when One rewrites and reprograms One's living operating system. The key is overturning One's limiting beliefs and realising One's infinite potential at this moment as a spiritual Being in the universe. Everyone in the world can do this, one person at a time. Like filling an empty lake with individual raindrops from the sky. At first One may feel alone, but after a little time, One will be joined by others and begin to experience life as part of a pool of positive possibilities. This will in turn attract more and more raindrops until the lake overflows with incredible abundance and new life.

Eventually, over time, this spiritual path or divine direction will lead to society changing itself from the inside out. It will give rise to a new way of living, working and being in the world today. It will enable the manifestation of a peaceful, abundant and awakened interstellar spiritually united Type 1 civilisation on Earth. Trust oneself to live One's full potential in this life – this is how One creates a new reality, new life and new future now.

Valuing oneself and being spirit-centric in this world

Wherever One goes, One's spirit is already there now. One cannot outrun the present moment. One is here forever more – today, tomorrow and in the future. This is why it is so important to honour and value oneself as a spiritual Being hosting a human form wherever One is at this moment in time.

If drama and stress seem to constantly fill One's life, maybe it is time to review and re-evaluate One's life, the people in it and the day-to-day choices that One is making on the planet. Know that there is a beautiful divine light within every Being on Earth.

Life is short. Focus on what truly matters the most in One's life. Change what and who you value to align with One's higher self in this world. It is time to give up all distractions and the things which stifle One's excitement, joy and celebration of life. Learn to make One's life priorities One's living mission and life outcome now.

Stop and ask oneself these very important questions: Does whatever One is doing now value add to One's spirit, relationships, purpose or life goals? Is it adding to One's quality of life at this moment? If One answers 'yes', continue doing it. But if the answer is 'no', stop whatever One is doing and change One's thoughts, beliefs and actions immediately.

With the courage to act, One's future vision and dreams will manifest today.

Just because One has not figured it all out doesn't mean that One needs to give up and stop believing in oneself or do nothing in life. Make an effort with everything that One thinks, does and speaks. Act mindfully and purposefully by aligning One's thoughts, habits, behaviours and actions in coherence with One's mind–body–spirit. Imagine the destination, but focus on the next step of One's life journey now. Every new day is another day to start over and have another go at being the best version of oneself in this world. Listen in silence as One's spirit speaks to oneself. Allow its message to touch One's inner heart and its wisdom to fill One's mind like a gentle breeze on a summer day.

As a person with infinite potential, do not judge oneself for making mistakes or stumbling along One's path in life. Always give oneself time to learn, time to change, time to grow, heal and reinvent oneself. Then create space in One's life to simply move on with care, kindness, and compassion. Be confident that One has seized the moment to become a better person today.

Just in case One has forgotten to remind oneself this today: One's spirit is perfect, One's body is an expression of life, One's mind is a beautiful paradise, One's inner light, love and oneness are connected to the entire universe, One is worthy and enough, and One is doing an amazing job at flowing with life as it unfolds in the direction of One's higher self now. One is capable of incredible things in this world, especially when One has a deeper and more profound spiritual relationship with oneself and others in One's life. When One is able to bring the cosmic light of One's spiritual presence into the moment with another living entity on the planet, One adds value to this person's or entity's existence and, at the same time, One value adds to oneself.

Teach oneself not to chase after external validation or attention to add value to One's life. Instead, act without expectation and watch how One can attract value into One's own life by adding value to others first.

One can only give what One has got. This is the formula for 'paying it forward' to others in the world. Simply unconditionally give and be an observer or a witness of this giving process.

Then watch how this act of generosity facilitates and influences a sense of growth or a giving mindset in others. When each person adopts the virtue of generosity in One's life, it creates a positive flow of energy out into the world. It creates a shared experience for all. The more One is able to give, the greater the gift of giving will be in this world. This has a direct impact on people's experiences of prosperity, abundance and self-realisation. It is also an important part of the 'awakening process' happening now on Earth.

As time moves on, One will be able to see and experience more and more great disclosures of the truth on the planet. As a reader of this book, One is already contributing to raising the current level of spiritual consciousness to a higher level of existence on the planet. One's spiritual and psychic energy is adding value to creating a new reality where people are living in an interstellar spiritually united Type 1 civilisation on the planet. The window of change is already here now as people peer through the looking glass into the future.

Take a moment to review and read this affirmation to manifest One's living future on Earth:

Affirmation to manifest One's living future on Earth

One agrees and says 'yes' to any and all contracts, agreements, relationships, alliances, partnerships, friendships, allegiances, communications and coherent (mind–body–spirit) consciousness energy exchanges with any and all persons, sentient Beings, extraterrestrials or spiritual entities in the universe that positively support the co-creation of an interstellar spiritually united Type 1 civilisation on Earth now to benefit all future generations of humanity living in peace, harmony and balance on the planet.

One understands with absolute clarity that the relationship that One has with oneself sets the whole tone for every other relationship that One has in One's life now. The day that One makes oneself a priority in One's own life is the day that One will begin to see great things start to change and new opportunities manifest or appear in front of One. One knows that the universe is always on One's side – today, tomorrow, forever.

When One unequivocally believes in oneself as spirit, soul or cosmic consciousness. One will create a paradigm shift within the mental matrix of One's mind and inner spiritual consciousness. One will open a divine porthole or cosmic gateway to the universe. One will be able to add value to One's life and living existence on the planet simply by perceiving oneself as a worthy Being. One will also recognise oneself as an integral part of the universe.

Through learning who One is and loving who this is now, One will be nurturing and living a spirit-centric life in the world.

In order to be fully engaged in this world, One must take time to recharge, raise One's vibrations and destress from the pressures of everyday life.

There are many types of rest, recovery and renewal that can add value to One's life on Earth.

Mental

Give oneself a break from thinking or overthinking things. Create space in One's life for inner peace, tranquillity and calmness within One's mind. Learn to continually let go of any and all negative thoughts and energy throughout the day.
- Practice mindful meditation (20 minutes per day).
- Ground oneself by touching the Earth and Country (land, sea and sky).
- Simply breathe – take long slow breaths and just relax now.
- Learn to be silent and do nothing.

Physical

Release stress and muscle tension through passive and active nurturing and healing.
- Do yoga or simple stretching exercises.
- Take a gentle walk or just wander freely without a deadline.
- Enjoy a relaxing massage or take a warm soothing bath.
- Sit in a peaceful place or just listen to soothing music.
- Go to bed early to ensure plenty of quality sleep.

Emotional

Surrender One's emotions to Source or the universe to reduce feelings of being emotionally overwhelmed by people, situations or circumstances.
- Take time to journal One's feelings: 'I let go of these feelings of [insert feelings] to Source and the universe knowing One is safe, loved and supported'.
- Go to a place where One can be quiet, calm and peaceful – i.e. no noise or distractions.
- Learn to say 'no thanks' or 'no – I'm not currently available'.
- Be with supportive friends or family and share One's feelings in a safe space without judgement
- Allow space and time for One's emotions to simply pass through One like a wave moving across the ocean

Spiritual

Align with One's inner spirit and connect with the universe.
- Meditate in a quiet space at home or in nature or do some 'nature bathing'.
- Focus on One's spiritual presence in this life now.
- Write or read spiritual affirmations that support the coherence of One's mind–body–spirit.
- Create some alone time and spend a whole day in complete silence – not speaking or texting anyone.

Social

Ensure plenty of space for quality-of-life activities, self-care and downtime to just chill out.
- Give oneself a treat to reward and celebrate key milestones in One's life.
- Go to the bush, beach, park, forest or conservation reserve for a walk or simply sit and enjoy life in the natural environment – soak in the vibration of nature and harmonise with it.
- Take oneself on an outing to the movies or go to a local café for breakfast or morning tea/brunch/lunch.
- Have a personal self-care day at a spa or resort to pamper oneself.
- Invest in One's personal grooming by getting a haircut, manicure, pedicure, facial, etc.

Creative

Release oneself from the pressure to create new things or solutions and give oneself a break.
- Take a tea-coffee break and sit in complete silence (mini meditation for 5 to 10 minutes).
- Go for a short walk, step outside and move One's body (incidental exercise).
- Enjoy the sights and sounds of nature or a garden.
- Do nothing and just breathe now.

Sensory

Turn off all electronic devices and put down One's smartphone to give One's mind–body some rest from the white noise of modern society.
- Turn off technology and tune into One's inner spirit, soul or cosmic consciousness.
- Plan and take a trip into nature, Country or the natural environment.
- Pamper oneself with a massage or full body spa treatment.
- Light a candle or incense or diffuse essential oils.
- Close One's eyes and listen to some relaxing peaceful music or soothing sounds in nature.

It is important that whatever One decides to do, One focuses on value-adding to One's life on the planet through life-enhancing thoughts and actions that nurture and nourish One's mind–body–spirit. The way to do this is to develop simple habits and positive patterns in One's life that emphasise and celebrate One's spirit-centric existence on Earth.

With everything One thinks, believes and does, One is creating One's vibrational alignment to this reality in this world. The future is therefore a function of One's present integrated resonance, not One's past.

Knowing the right signs, connections and relationships in One's life

Knowing the right signs, connections and relationships in one's life can bring about many positive benefits, from an increase in personal growth to greater unity and collective learning. As humanity continues to evolve and grow as a species, this knowledge will become increasingly important in helping One to navigate the challenges everyone faces and build a brighter future for all of humankind.

Here are some of the ways in which this knowledge and way of living life can assist and support humanity to evolve on Earth individually and collectively, ultimately leading to a spiritually united Type 1 civilisation.

Personal growth

Knowing the right signs, connections, and relationships in one's life can help individuals to grow personally and spiritually. This knowledge can help One understand One's purpose in life, the direction One should be headed in and the kind of relationships, partnerships and connections that will support One's individual growth.

Emotional social support

Having the right connections and relationships can provide emotional and social support when it is needed most. This is especially important during difficult times when One needs someone to lean on and help One successfully navigate the common challenges faced by all people.

Collaborative happenings

When people come together with a shared vision, common purpose and an intentional outcome, they can achieve great things. Knowing the right connections, way and relationships can help facilitate these collaborations, leading to amazing positive change in the world.

Collective learnings

As individuals connect with one another, One can learn from each other's experiences and knowledge, leading to collective learning and growth. This can be especially important when it comes to solving complex problems that require diverse perspectives and alternative approaches.

Greater spiritual unity

When individuals connect with one another in meaningful and spiritual ways, it can lead to greater spiritual unity and a sense of shared purpose on the planet. This helps bring people together across cultural and geographical boundaries, leading to a spiritually united Type 1 civilisation.

When One is living in a different frequency and energetic vibration, One will notice that One is automatically attracted to certain individuals, places and practices in life. There will be people that One just 'clicks' with, while others will be out of sync with oneself. Do not worry. This is a normal experience for people operating at a higher level of consciousness in the community and the world today.

Much of the time, others will be unable to comfortably connect, hear what One is saying or understand the message that One is freely giving. This is because they can only meet One at the same depth in which they have met oneself first. An egoic or closed mind will always be bound by its self-defined limits and social constraints.

Do not be discouraged if this is the situation or if some people just naturally drift away from One's friendship circle or stop being part of One's social peers. It is inevitable that this will happen at some point in One's life.

Let go of trying to continually 'fix' things or invest energy into explaining who One is now and why One is on this inner path of self-awareness and 'spiritual awakening'. Some people will 'get it' but there are others that, no matter how One explains it, will not be able to understand One's new path, direction and lifestyle.

Know that One is a limitless Being of the cosmos with infinite potential to do anything and go anywhere in the universe. One is not defined by human laws or conditioned mind patterns of the past, reactive responses, low-level emotions, negative energy or self-defeating behaviours, habits or beliefs. One is so much more than this limited human concept of oneself in this life. One is an integral part of the universe, a changeless, limitless and ever-present observer of all that exists now.

Every time that One chooses to be present is a choice that One is making to be true to oneself. One is accepting oneself as spirit, soul or cosmic consciousness. When One does this, it creates an inner mind–body–spirit coherence that is vibrating in alignment with One's higher self as a Being of light, love and oneness.

It is in this state that One is able to bring great clarity to One's life journey on Earth. Within this clear vision is where One will find a way to see the future and bring it into the present moment. One will also be able to transcend time and space itself. Know that the right path, right person and right connections will come to One – just be patient now. The universe is working with One to bring all that is needed to fulfil One's life purpose on Earth here today.

Whenever an issue, concern or worry comes into One's life, follow these five simple steps to create a living solution and move on with care, kindness, compassion and confidence.

 **Stay present in the moment**

Focus on being in a state of divine coherence – mind-body-spirit.

 **Be openly non-judgemental**

One is not the issue, concern or problem being experienced now. Remove oneself from the equation of life or challenge before One. Create space (distance) between oneself and the 'problem'. Chill out, relax and be open-minded from an objective viewpoint.

 **Simply observe with curiosity**

Whatever it is – it is what it is, nothing more and nothing less. Attach no meaning or attribute any value to the issue, concern or worry. See it as simply the chaos of life presenting itself or reorganising itself in front of One now. Do not internalise or externalise the 'challenge' or 'problem'. Look at it without any emotional reaction, judgement or personal bias – stay calm, quiet and at peace from a place of One's spirit, soul or cosmic consciousness.

 **Be silently non-reactive**

Stay in a space of non-reactive stillness or observable neutrality. Practice being virtuous and respond from a field of pure potentiality. Say to oneself and others, 'How can One help or be helpful?'

 **Trust in the universe**

Flow with life and the process of change. Be receptive and welcome a creative solution, as it will surely emerge. Activate One's intuitive intelligence and divine knowing in silent meditation. The answer or solution will always manifest itself in the present moment.

As soon as you honour the present moment, unhappiness and struggle dissolve, and life begins to flow with joy and ease.
Eckhart Tolle

Know that the universe is giving One signs, hints and tips for living a spiritual life and experiencing a wonderful lifestyle every day. The universe is in continual conversation with oneself, it is occurring:
- while One is resting or sleeping
- at breakfast, lunch and dinner or when One is going out
- when One is completing simple or complex tasks
- in meditation or going for a morning walk
- along One's journey to places and on One's daily path in life
- in conversations with oneself and others
- while using IT or AI platforms and feeds on social media
- on Country (land, sea and sky)
- in the synchronicities that One encounters throughout the day.

Pay attention to these pieces of information, recognise the patterns and form a coherent inclusive thought. Know that the universe is always on and communicating with One in a way that aligns with One's spirit, soul or cosmic consciousness.

It is time to free One's mind and open One's heart to intuitively look, listen and learn about all the signs, signals and simple ways in which the universe and One's own spirit guides One along 'the way'.

Many people think that a sign is something big, but in most cases it is small, subtle and a gentle nudge to 'look this way', 'go this way' or 'give way' so that a thing may occur or present itself in the moment.

The way forward to living an awakened life begins the moment One realises that One is the creator of One's reality and can choose any path to positive prosperity or amazing abundance. Make a conscious and brave decision to lean into One's fear and boldly confront the dragon of dishonesty, deception and danger in One's mind. Learn to be honest with oneself in the way that One perceives One's current reality and relationships on the planet. Some relationships will be hurtful or harmful, while others will be helpful and hopeful. Choose what type of relationship One seeks to have with oneself, others and the universe. Life is an opportunity to co-create or manifest the dream that One thinks One is worthy of living now. Imagine only the best for oneself in every moment of One's life. Believe that everything will work out for One and it will.

Know that every person is on One's own life journey on this planet. Everyone everywhere is simply seeking a way to be in alignment with One's inner spirit, soul or cosmic consciousness and find One's way home to Source.

For everyone that comes into One's life, there will be someone that leaves it. Welcome the time that One spends with others along One's life journey here on Earth. Friends, family, lovers and partners will all be present when it is One's time to reconnect with these individuals.

Simply stay open, be present now and move along 'the way' that welcomes One's spiritual evolution on Earth.

Transcending One's human living operating system

Transcending One's human living operating system and evolving spiritually is significant because it can help to unlock One's full potential, find greater meaning and a sense of purpose in life. It also helps and assists One to become a more loving, kind and compassionate human being in this world.

The human living operating system is like the software that runs on a computer. It consists of our beliefs, values, virtues, habits and ways of thinking that guide our actions and decisions. While this operating system helps us navigate the world, it also limits our potential and can prevent us from experiencing a deeper sense of fulfillment and purpose.

Transcending One's human living operating system means breaking free from the limitations of One's current beliefs and ways of thinking and opening oneself up to new experiences and possibilities. This allows One to tap into a higher sense of consciousness, which can lead to a greater understanding of oneself, others and the world around One now.

Spiritual evolution is the process of expanding One's awareness and deepening One's connection to something greater than oneself. By transcending One's human living operating system and evolving spiritually, One can gain a greater sense of inner peace, joy and purpose, and become a more compassionate, empathetic, and loving human being. This, in turn, can help One create a better world for oneself and all others on Earth.

To be in a different state of mind or go beyond the range or limits of One's current perspective, conceptual sphere, reality or field of activity or experience, One will need to change the way One looks at it now. When One changes how One looks at things, the things that One is looking at also change too. This is all part of affecting the quantum unified field of reality or expressed spiritual consciousness in which One exists. Changing One's perception shifts the probability of how things appear to be and create new possibilities of an altered potential reality.

I am life. I am the space in which all things happen. I am consciousness. I am the now.
Eckhart Tolle

As One becomes fully present now with One's cosmic divinity as a sentient Being of the universe, One will be able to shift into a higher state and experience alternative dimensions of One's existence. One will be able to go beyond the current limitation of 3D space–time and peer into the future as if it is happening now.

Transcending One's human living operating system is not the major issue that most people perceive it to be. Everyone on the planet can do it. One simply needs to answer One's inner spiritual call to action and choose to change. With this choice, One will begin a process of consciously evolving on this planet into the Being that One is destined to be now.

The process is easy. One just needs to come to terms with One's human mortality and spiritual infinite existence in this world, and realise that One must free oneself from the mental matrix and conditioned ego-centric cultural programming of One's own mind in this society.

It is time to stop thinking about One's endless problems, issues, concerns or worries. All this wasted energy only serves One's ego in affirming that One is not deserving or worthy enough. One must end the procrastination preventing One from taking direct action in One's own life on the planet. One does this by knowing that One is on an important mission to repurpose, refocus and recommit oneself to a new manifested reality on Earth now. A new and beautiful future that is about taking One's rightful spiritual place in this world and amongst the stars.

To do this, One will need to decommission One's old human living operating system and upgrade it now. Removing or deleting old thoughts, habits and beliefs will require One to create new space in One's life and mind to co-create a better future for oneself now. It will necessitate moving or shifting away from outdated or obsolete personal practices, familiar behaviours and long-held beliefs. It is time to adapt to a new future by altering One's thoughts, reconfiguring One's energy and creating change in every aspect of One's life.

Being in sync with One's spirit and life on this planet means living in synchronicity with the universe – it is that simple.

> **The best way to predict the future is to fold this alternative reality into the present moment now.**

Resistance to change will only cause ongoing stress and suffering in this world. It is possible to move towards being spiritually enlightened or awake in the universe by simply staying silent and being in complete coherence within oneself – mind–body–spirit. But it is not possible to personally grow, change and evolve without some degree of disruptive discontinuity and challenging discomfort in One's life.

The key to moving forward while staying present is as much an art as it is a mindful practice. The best way is to first align with One's spirit, soul or spiritual consciousness and then intuitively navigate a truly enlightened or awake path using One's internal spiritual intelligence. Realise that One as a spirit is a divine wave from the infinite ocean of existence in this universe.

Use every encounter with others as a learning or teaching moment. All people are One's peers in how to be a better version of oneself. Become a student of life and live it in such a way that it aligns with the seven key virtues (compassion, helpfulness, acceptance, generosity, simplicity, patience and openness) and with One's mind–body–spirit.

To adjust One's life trajectory and point it in a different direction. One must change the programming within One's internal living operating system. One does this by reconfiguring One's thoughts to align with One's higher self. This automatically shifts the divine consciousness and unified field of One's living presence in the world today.

Start by simply changing one single thought and follow it with one simple action. This is how lakes and oceans around the world are filled – one raindrop at a time.

Know that One has the power to change and, with this change, repurpose, refocus and recommit One's life to become the best version of oneself. All One has to do is begin where One is now. Do not wait for someone or something to come along to tell oneself what to do. Reading the words on the pages of this book is a sign that One is destined for change and will co-create something special with One's life.

Every thought that One has ever had since being born as a human on this planet can be changed now. There are no limits in this world except for those that One places on oneself at this moment.

Take a break and step out of the contemporary chaos in One's life. Look around and observe with mindful practice the structure of One's mind, thoughts and feelings. Know that as a spiritual Being One is not One's thoughts and that every thought is only a temporary construct in space–time. It is only there to fulfil a single purpose as part of the living process.

The way to let go and shift One's living operating system is to become completely detached from One's existing outdated and obsolete thoughts. The thoughts that have led oneself where One is today are not the same thoughts that will co-create oneself to enable a new future reality on Earth. One must wake up now and rewire One's brain in order to manifest a new destiny that aligns with One's higher spiritual self.

This kind of inner work takes time, commitment and practice. When One works on oneself, One will start to notice incredible things come into synchronicity in One's life. It is as if these new thoughts, feelings and experiences were already purposely designed for oneself. As One begins to change One's energetic vibrational field or resident energy signature, it will create a ripple effect wherever One is in the world. One will be drawn to new people, new paths and new experiences in life. These things will also be attracted to

One too. One will notice that solutions to problems will appear before One as if like magic. In addition, One is no longer concerned with the old ways of living. One will begin to reject and turn away from people, situations and experiences that promote an ego-centric lifestyle and meaningless life in this world.

The shifting of One's beliefs and inner thoughts reshapes the world that One lives in today. When One finally experiences a paradigm shift in One's thinking, it will be like walking across a cosmic bridge into a completely new world. One will have purposely and intentionally created a new spiritual lens to observe and view the world that One lives in now.

It is within this new pure consciousness that One is destined to be and exist in this present moment. Nothing can alter the fact that One has altered One's living reality by upgrading One's human living operating system so that it aligns with One's spirit, soul or cosmic consciousness. One will feel, think, behave and act differently as One becomes spiritually centred.

This is all part of the spiritual evolutionary process happening now on Earth. Every person is part of the wakening and the wakening is part of the lives of everyone on the planet (even if unawaken people are not yet aware of it).

IMPORTANT LEARNINGS, TEACHINGS AND POINTINGS

Key ways to live life as spirit, soul or cosmic consciousness

01 One's divine purpose on this planet is to be consciously awake now.

02 When One is truly present, One does not need to force anything to happen in life. All One needs to do is surrender, have faith and observe as everything unfolds perfectly for One. Know that One has the 'power of presence' to influence, shift and shape the current reality of One's life and the lives of others in this world.

03 Take radical responsibility to transform One's own level of consciousness so that it operates at an increased frequency in alignment with One's higher spiritual self. This can be achieved when One rewrites and reprograms One's human living operating system. The key is overturning One's limiting beliefs and realising One's infinite potential at this moment as a spiritual Being in the universe.

04 Do not chase after external validation or attention to add value to One's life. Instead, act without expectation and watch how One is able to attract value into One's own life by adding value to others first.

 Know that One is a limitless Being of the cosmos with infinite potential to do anything and go anywhere in the universe. The right path, right person and right connections will come to One – stay focused on the outcome and be patient.

 To adjust One's life trajectory and point it in a different direction to where One is heading now, One must change the programming within One's internal human living operating system. Know that the spiritual evolutionary process is happening now on Earth. Every person is part of 'the wakening' (even if they are not aware of it).

PART SIX

Transfigure life, the universe and everything

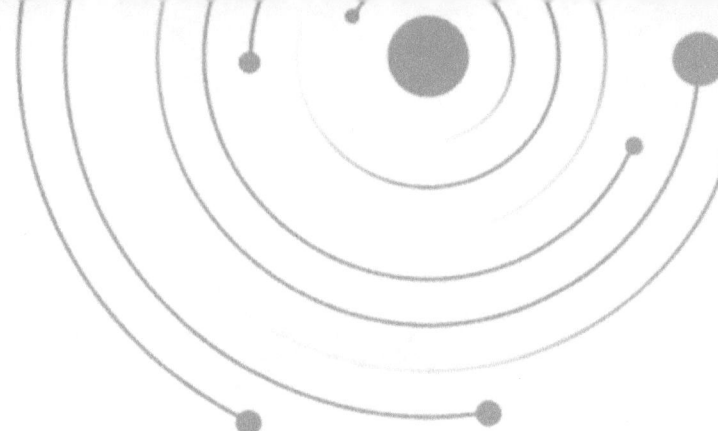

Affecting great change now in One's life and on Earth

To transfigure life, the universe and everything is to transform it into something more beautiful or elevated in this world. Simply begin wherever One is now.

In giving effect to this idea and future vision, One needs to perceive an altered reality where One can see, sense and be in sync with this new spiritual outcome about how One will live life on Earth.

One must look and change within oneself. This inner way will naturally and usually transform One's outer world for the better. In most circumstances, it may mean that One will have to get slightly uncomfortable with change and growth so that One is able to transition to a new way of thinking, speaking, acting, seeing, perceiving and believing in the world that One currently lives in now.

Do not resist change – embrace One's fear and let it pass over One until there is nothing left but the essence of One's immortal and infinite Being. Letting go of what One has previously learnt as a child, young person or adult is all part of the process of evolving into a Being of light, love and oneness on the planet. Realising that One's pre-existing sociocultural programming, conditioned thinking and 'old world beliefs' are outdated, past their use-by date and obsolete, is an important aspect in coming to terms with the fact that One needs to change now.

The more One can let go, the more One will be able to co-create a different and more spiritually aligned future for oneself in this world. Freedom does not come from some other person giving oneself permission to be free, but from the intention to free oneself from all things that One is attached to now. The more that One can live, work, play and rest within a state of coherence (mind–body–spirit), the greater One will be able to effect positive change within oneself and influence the world around One.

Seek not to accumulate more material items, money or engage in the latest social fad, season's fashion or fabricated ego-centric 'new life' or 'get rich quick' scam. Recognise when others approach oneself with false promises and fake intentions. These people carry a distinct vibrational energy signature of deception, deceit and dishonesty. Learn to read the signs and become aware of One's intuition when encountering these people. Look at the so-called appointed and democratic leaders in the community and society who say one thing and yet do another. A good leader will not seek to be rewarded in such a way that it strokes his or her ego. A great leader is called to action and answers the call. These people stand out because they stand behind people in the aspiration of accomplishing something greater than oneself. Supporting, encouraging, suggesting, praising and practicing the seven key virtues (compassion, helpfulness, acceptance, generosity, simplicity, patience and openness).

> **No single person is perfect in this world and yet this world is perfect for everyone.**

The only perfection that One will find is within the pure divinity of One's infinite existence in the universe.

All spiritual Beings on the planet are on a spiritual journey to return to Source. This life is very short and, as such, it should be treated with unending humility, overflowing awe and living gratitude for the time that One is here on Earth. Do not expect other people to do the right thing in this life. Learn to sense other's energy, note other's living intentions and committed actions. Act without any external assumptions about what a person may or may not do. Trust in the universe and have faith that everything will work out okay. Do not pay particular attention to the unkind, cruel and criminal things that are currently happening around the world today.

The way to influence, inspire and instil great positivity and an abundance of optimism in the world is to first become these things. Radiate the divine light, cosmic wisdom and positive energy within One's sentient Being out into the world. Take action with One's own spiritual thoughts, words, presence, habits, behaviours and actions.

Most people are familiar with the phrase, 'With great power comes great responsibility'. However, there is also another important saying that One is fond of too. 'With simple action, comes significant change.'

Learn to change One thought at a time, then turn this thought into action and keep moving forward in this way. A thought is just a thought and can be changed at any time or any place on the planet. One did not sign a contract with the universe whereby One is required to think the same thoughts, believe the same things or behave the same way as One did five minutes, five hours or five days ago. One can choose to change One's mind–body and spiritually evolve now.

As One evolves on the planet, One will notice oneself moving away from people with ego-centric agendas and towards people with spirit-centric intentions. What some people see as fixed within families, communities, societies and First Nations is nothing more than an illusion trapped within the cultural scaffolding of the past or current conditioned thinking of the present. All that appears is an illusion. All illusions appear to be real to a mind that is blind to them. Every person with an egoic mind will only see what it wants to see in this life. This type of person does not want the illusion of One's life to be shattered, smashed or destroyed. A person with this kind of mindless lifestyle will do everything to stop the illusion from ending, no matter how it affects, harms or hurts others. However, this is the exact thing that One must do in order to escape the self-imposed prison within One's own mind and see the truth.

The truth is that One is spirit, soul or cosmic consciousness first and a human being second, not the other way around. One is host to One's human form for a limited time before returning to Source. One is not here by chance but by divine choice to awaken and live a purposeful life here and now. One is powerful beyond measure. One is an integral part of the universe itself as an infinite, immortal and eternal Being of love, light and oneness.

This truth will likely resonate deeply within One's own Being as One reads these words. The messages within this book are as timeless, endless and boundless as One's Being is in the universe. There is a certain 'isness' to One's existence in this life and One's journey across the vastness of the universe. When One is truly present now, One is able to see beyond the illusion of life into the cosmic reality of divine existence.

Believing in the future is an act of faith in the present moment now. One realises that whatever One is thinking, doing and speaking to at this moment, One is giving energy to manifesting this occurrence as a tangible reality now.

To co-create change in One's life, the world and the universe, One will need to create space within oneself first to do so. The universe cannot exist without the consciousness of space and space for altered consciousness.

> **Everything arises out of nothing, and nothing exists within everything.**

This is how all things can exist in the universe – every relationship One will ever have in this world and on this planet is impermanent.

This is the paradox of conscious existence in the universe.

It is important to know that whatever One seeks in this life is also seeking oneself too. This is the synchronicity of the universe expressing itself through all things, all points in space and time, and all moments that One exists in now – in the past and the future. One is spiritually entangled with every other sentient Being in the universe at this present moment. As One moves towards the future on this planet, One is also converging on a point of spiritual singularity in space–time on Earth. One is unable to stop it, like the rain falling from the sky or the divine act of creation itself. One is intuitively and instinctively guided along 'the way' to the end, the beginning and the Source of all truth in the universe.

Simply accept that One is part of this 'great awakening' and awaken completely within oneself now.

Trusting oneself, One's spirit and the universe

Some people find it very hard to trust others because One has been hurt, betrayed or let down time and time again by people that One implicitly trusted. Living through and surviving this kind of experience can be a powerful turning point in One's life. Some people are left significantly scarred while others use this interpersonal exchange of energies as a point of motivation to inspire oneself.

When One is able to see any and all human experiences through a lens that is without judgement or attachment, One is ready to move on with One's life. Sometimes this will require One to undertake a healing journey to unconditionally look at, accept, release, reconfigure and resolve any adverse impacts that have occurred to One's mind–body. Any pain that One may have experienced is a sign that One needs to pay particular attention to this area within One's mind or body.

It is inevitable that every person on the planet will experience some form of psychological, social or physical pain in One's life. But this does not mean that this experience will necessarily create ongoing suffering over the course of the rest of a person's lifetime. Pain is often required for One's personal growth especially when One is transitioning from a baby to a child and then into a teenager, young adult and finally into adulthood. Personal pain is usually seen as a symptom or sign that something is 'wrong', changing or disrupting One's human form 'normal' functioning.

When One can view pain through a self-learning, ongoing quality improvement process and the living lens of inner wisdom, One will be able to grow more smoothly and create greater awareness in One's life. This is a sure sign that One is beginning to trust oneself.

Learning to trust oneself is all about listening to One's spiritual intuition. One does this by simply being present with One's spirit, soul or cosmic consciousness in every aspect of One's life. From the time that One wakes up in the morning to the time that One finally falls asleep at night, One needs to realise that One is walking the Earth as a spiritual Being in a human form and not the other way around. Recognising and acknowledging that One is a sentient Being of the infinite cosmos is the beginning point to having a true divine relationship with the universe.

Trusting oneself, One's spirit and the universe requires One to take a leap of faith. When One finally does this, a great gateway of opportunity will be opened for oneself to explore and experience new things in this life, world and universe. It is not about having all the pieces to the puzzle of life already figured out. It is learning to believe that everything will work out for One in the end, no matter what happens.

Creating an inner belief that is supportive of oneself relies on establishing some founding principles of self-worth, self-care, self-awareness and self-investment. Wherever One is now and whatever One is doing at this moment in time, One has the power to change to become the best version of oneself in this lifetime. Just because One did something in the past does not mean that One must continue to do the same thing in the future. Old habits, behaviours and thought patterns that no longer serve oneself today will need to be removed from One's living operating system. The quickest and easiest way to do this is to be truly honest with oneself now. As difficult as this may appear to be, One needs to let go of all the things that vibrate at a lower level of consciousness.

The concept and idea of fear or any fearful thoughts will always vibrate at a lower level within One's mind–body. If One holds on to such things, it will create a mental matrix of limitation, control and constraint within the structure of One's mind. Recognising One's own fear is part of the process of self-awareness. It allows One to observe One's mind and the thoughts that are contained within it. It is important to realise that as a spirit, One is not bound by the thoughts that One thinks within One's human mind. Therefore, with the right intuitive insight and motivational incentive, One can break One's own sociocultural programming and conditioned neural pathways in One's brain and evolve on the planet.

This process of evolution for most human beings can be somewhat incremental and at other times it can be quite disruptive or significantly abrupt – even brutal. Whatever form this evolving process takes, know that One's spirit will never be harmed, hurt or injured. This is why One is able to trust oneself that, in the end, everything will be okay. However, getting to this point may require One's mind–body to undergo slight or significant reconfiguration of 'the self'.

It is highly likely that what One perceives as 'the self' or One's human identity will be completely dismantled, dissolved or destroyed. This may come as an incredible shock to most people, but what One thinks as the concept of 'you' or 'myself' or 'me' will no longer be relevant after One has spiritually evolved into a higher state of existence on the planet. Trust One when One says that the 'you' or 'persona' which One has been carefully grooming and crafting over the past years and decades will not exist beyond this point of emergence.

One's life will be defined or reorganised in two ways. First, the years and decades when One was asleep and identifying with One's human form and egoic identity. Second, the time after One's awakening when One aligned One's existence on the planet to One's true identity as a spiritual Being of the universe.

The tipping point for all personal change is different for everyone on Earth. Some are able to trust One's spirit at an early age because One has been exposed to or grew up in a culture, community and society where parents, family and friends talked openly about spirit, soul or cosmic consciousness. However, One may have had an experience when this spiritual messaging was suppressed, hidden or even legally banned by the governing powers in order to maintain an egoic agenda and ruling class of people or wealthy elites in society.

The invention of computers, the internet and smartphones have increased ordinary people's access to global information, communication and networking with each other all around the planet. This greater connectivity is leading to an exponential sharing of people's thoughts on social media along with the formation of networks of people who share a similar interest in raising the level of spiritual consciousness of all Beings on Earth.

As human beings begin to spiritually trust oneself and other humans in the world, this will give rise to a new shared social scaffolding for the networking of global trust with like-minded, spirit-centric people. This new networking of ideas, energies and interests will expand and eventually cover the entire planet. It will become a form of neural linking of minds and support the creation of a shared collective consciousness between all spiritually awake sentient Beings on the planet.

Trusting oneself, One's spirit and the universe is key to how human evolution will work to co-create an interstellar spiritually united Type 1 civilisation on Earth now. Individual micro changes and networks are already being formed to facilitate this new future reality on Earth today. Without realising it, an event horizon is fast approaching humanity that will sweep away the years and decades of egoic misinformation, indoctrination and control to unveil a new way of living, working, playing and being in the world.

> The more One is able to reduce, remove and repurpose fear, the greater One will be able to create a space for love, trust and light to be present in every aspect of One's life.

As One becomes the change that One seeks, this change will be manifested in One's life now.

Altering, adjusting and adapting when things aren't working out

There is no shame in admitting when things are simply not working out for oneself. It is important to ask others for help when One needs or requires it. The trick is knowing when and how to do this. The divine Source for all things does not expect One to know everything in the universe only to be present where One is now. The universe exists as an infinite intelligence and ubiquitous entity. It already is omnipresent, omnipotent, omniscience and omnibenevolent. The is-ness of its existence is all part of the universe being in an infinite awakened state.

> For every issue, concern, worry or problem in One's life, an answer or a solution already exists within One's spiritual consciousness. Simply access it now.

Learning how to read the signs is the key to understanding how to choose the right path, in the right moment, that will lead One along the right way to the right outcome. If One has intentionally or unintentionally walked oneself into a difficult situation in a relationship, at work, in debt, with a family member or in life in general, One can also walk oneself out of it too. Nothing is fixed in this world, not even One's current attachment to a perceived, actual or potential issue, concern or problem. One has the power to change One's thoughts, beliefs, habits, and actions and thus shift One's direction and ultimate trajectory in life.

Do not underestimate One's ability to refocus, reshape and recommit One's life to a new reality on Earth. Everything that One has learnt to date has led oneself to this moment. However, it can all change and move in a beautiful, wonderful and enlightened direction if One chooses to align with One's higher self.

One's mission or overall life goal is not about getting something, but about waking up to being someone of significance in an awakened state of existence on the planet. Most of the mainstream media manufacture artificial images and false facts designed to illicit a reaction based on fear. This taps directly into One's ego and invokes a 'reactive fear response'. In essence, mainstream media is for the most part an addictive visual information factory designed to serve an egoic paradigm of fear, hate, loss, scarcity, control and separateness.

Many humans in the past hundred years since the invention of television have become victims of this agenda, believing that what One saw as news or stories about current affairs on the nightly television was 'real' or in some ways 'truth reporting'. Unfortunately, this was a boldface and blatant lie. The motivation to produce this information was in part to mislead, misinform and manipulate the minds of the masses in one way or another. Do not feel angry or disappointed that One has fallen victim to this corporate greed and subtle suppressive social agenda. It is all about maintaining the status quo in 'keeping people ignorant' of One's spirit, soul or cosmic consciousness. In doing this, it allowed a social system to be created that supported the investment in and championing of the 'Rule of Ego' in the lives of everyday citizens in the world and across the planet.

The Rule of Ego can be summarised in the following egoic principles, codes of conduct and ways of living One's life:

> **Egoic principles, codes of conduct and ways of living One's life**
>
> 1. Attachment to greed, lust and power
> 2. Continually judging other people and situations
> 3. Seeking ongoing attention and validation
> 4. Constantly comparing oneself to others
> 5. Desperately craving respect and recognition
> 6. Always being defensive, reactive and adversarial
> 7. Setting unrealistic and unattainable goals
> 8. Acting selfishly and rarely (if ever) helping others
> 9. Manipulating or controlling others to get what One wants

By aligning with the 'Rule of Ego' within One's mind, One has unconsciously adopted an egoic 'code of conduct' upon which to base One's point of reference and decision-making processes in the world. This kind of person will show or demonstrate the following traits.

> **Attachment to greed, lust and power**
>
> This type of person will believe that One can never have enough of something or someone in this life. There is no such thing as 'enough'. This person will be addicted to the sensation of more and more and still more material objects, money, power, people, physical/emotional pleasures, experiences or drug-induced highs. Greed will be One's operating program in life and One will never be able to satisfy this unquenchable desire in One's mind. This attachment will only lead to ongoing pain and suffering.
>
> **Note to self:** Be grateful and thankful for what One already has in this life (mind–body–spirit) and go from there.

Continually judging other people and situations

A person with this kind of outlook will always have an 'us vs them' or 'me against the world' attitude. One will be unable to congratulate others for One's good fortune, wealth, health, wellbeing, wellships or personal success in life because One will be thinking 'What about me?' or 'It's not fair!' One will have a constant fear of missing out (FOMO) about One's life. One will be unable to appreciate what is right in front of oneself. One will blame others and make all manner of excuses for One's personal circumstances or individual situation rather than taking any responsibility to improve, change oneself or One's life direction.

Note to self: Accept everything, everyone in every moment and judge nothing.

Seeking ongoing attention and validation

Attention seekers are likely to have low self-worth, an inflated sense of importance about oneself and a very strong desire for others to make One feel good about oneself. This kind of person believes that life is all about oneself and being at the centre of attention no matter what is happening (e.g. in a work meeting, at a friend's party, going out to dinner or the movies, during casual conversations in the workplace or community).

Note to self: Act without expectation. Actions speak louder than words; simply welcome praise when it arises. Focus on flowing with 'the way' of the universe to achieve the outcome in collaboration with other like-minded individuals.

Constantly comparing oneself to others

People who constantly compare oneself to others feel like One is somehow 'less than' other people and practice the habit of always devaluing oneself. One has uploaded and is operating with a deficit mindset, looking at the world from a 'glass half-empty' rather than a 'glass half-full' perspective. Here's the thing: comparing oneself only succeeds in reinforcing a lack of something within One's own internal value system. One will never be good enough for anything or anyone if One maintains this self-sabotaging thought stream in One's life.

Note to self: Focus on what One can control: One's thoughts, beliefs, actions and self-talk. One is a special sentient Being, a unique person and an integral part of the universe.

Desperately craving respect and recognition

Healthy relationships and good partnerships have a normal level of interpersonal respect and recognition. It is a natural outcome of people genuinely appreciating one another. People with an egoic code of conduct will distort these boundaries and always need to feel validated through excessive acts of respect, repetition and recognition. These types of people will go out of One's way to seek to be seen or rewarded in some way for what One is doing, even if it has no positive impact on a successful outcome.

Note to self: Know that One is enough – today, tomorrow and forever. Respect and recognition come after doing One's job successfully or a selfless act of kindness or compassion. Thanks is all One really needs in life.

Always being defensive, reactive and adversarial

A person with an egoic code of conduct will resist inner change and see any alternative thoughts, suggestions and actions as an 'assault' or 'attack' on One's personhood or individual identity. This type of person will always be in a defensive mode or posture, because One believes that other people are 'out to get One'. Standing on principle or being right is more important than developing good sound and healthy friendships, relationships, partnerships, wellships, a career or personal growth.

Note to self: Simply accept what is in this moment. Be open, actively listen and learn without interrupting or passing judgement – let the conversation flow. Take nothing personally; everyone is One's teacher. Adopt a continuous quality improvement mantra or philosophy to life to be the best version of oneself each and every day.

Setting unrealistic and unattainable goals

People with this kind of trait are often perfectionists full of pride about oneself and want to demonstrate a certain sense of superiority over others. This type of individual loves to show off how incredibly accomplished One is, brag about all the hard work that went into a project and gloat about One's success in life. This person desires to be known for an accomplishment and the rewards that come with achieving that goal.

Note to self: Redefine One's personal success to be from moment to moment – this is what really counts in life. Just do what needs to be done and let the universe take care of the rest.

Acting selfishly and rarely (if ever) helping others

People with an egoic interest in life tend to be very individualistic, selfish and self-serving. These individuals often disregard the needs of others and think only about satisfying oneself. This becomes the default cultural and social programming for One's life. People with this type of attitude have little meaningful social connections in the community and generally think that it's not worth One's time or effort to support others. One will have self-talk chatter in One's head that reinforces the 'What's in it for me?' approach to life. Most people who operate like this will lack any real sense of a social contract and be indifferent to the pain and suffering of others in the community or world. One's outlook in life will be focused and centred on increased wealth, fame, social status and an addiction to materialism.

Note to self: Working to fulfil or support the needs of others is often its own reward. Acting in the interests of someone else and helping this person can usually benefit many more people in the world.

Setting unrealistic and unattainable goals

People with this kind of trait are often perfectionists full of pride about oneself and want to demonstrate a certain sense of superiority over others. This type of individual loves to show off how incredibly accomplished One is, brag about all the hard work that went into a project and gloat about One's success in life. This person desires to be known for an accomplishment and the rewards that come with achieving that goal.

Note to self: Redefine One's personal success to be from moment to moment – this is what really counts in life. Just do what needs to be done and let the universe take care of the rest.

> ### Manipulating or controlling others
> ### to get what One wants
>
> This type of person is solely focused on doing whatever he or she wants with little or no regard for anybody else. One believes that One is entitled to anything or everything and is only concerned about getting it or getting there. One does not care about another person's feelings or how it will impact on a family member, friend, partner, lover, family, kin or community. One is addicted to the destination at all costs. One believes that One's life is more important than others and will do everything in One's power to coerce, deceive and manipulate someone into doing what One wants, getting the other person to believe what One is saying or simply use others for One's own needs – anytime, anywhere and anyhow.
>
> **Note to self: Actively remove egoic people from One's friendship circle. Stay centred within One's spirit, soul or cosmic consciousness and do not be sucked into a vortex of lies, toxicity, false truths and poisonous promises. Stay true to oneself, One's inner peace and One's spirit-centric way in the world.**

One may ask 'What does this have to do with things in One's life when they are not working out?' A major reason for things not working out in One's life is due to trying to live under, live within, live up to or serve the agenda of ego in One's life. Rather than living life in a spirit-centric way, most people live it in an ego-centric way. Over the past decades, most Western societies have purposely promoted an egoic culture and programming within its structures and institutions. This means that ever since the day One was born, One fully trusted One's caregivers, parents, family and society and believed that the information One was given was 'true and correct'. This unfiltered approach as a child resulted in fulling accepting that 'the ego' and egoic mental programs are the way that One needs to live One's life. The messaging has been that ego or egoic programming (i.e. greed, selfishness, self-interest, separateness, competition, conflict, battle, the adversarial legal system, majority democratic rule, survival of the fittest, slavery in all its forms, market-driven forces and growth economy) is good and the best way to have a fully functioning living social order or working modern society. But this is a blatant lie and a perversion of the truth.

This type of approach and arrangement is seen to work because it favours an egoic system of contemporary economic slavery over people as opposed to a spirit system of consciously aware relationships based on a shared prosperity and abundance model. A spirit-centric system promotes and enables traditional relationship values, inner virtues, spiritual honesty, integrity, authenticity, mutual respect, collective reciprocity and benevolent trade (win–win).

When living and operating within an egoic system, One often finds oneself resorting to and using egoic values, practices and processes in order to merely live and survive. This is why One can feel so out of sorts and often exhausted from continually having to compete, jostle, perform or fight for things, or ill or unwell. There is no overall goal or higher purpose for modern societies on the planet other than to manipulate people into a practice that promotes ongoing consumer materialism and the integrated economic slavery of the next generation.

This is why it is so important to become aware of One's ego and how it is affecting One's decision-making processes within One's mind so One can change and live a true, authentic and spiritual life.

If things are not working out, it may be simply because One is continuing to adopt an egoic framework or personal programming – trying to live life to meet the expectations of others, family, friends, kin or the community in which One lives in now. Ask oneself these questions:

- Is One experiencing specific, external reasons that things are not working out for oneself?
- Is One trying to meet another person's or other people's expectations?

- Is One driven by fear, greed or a selfish and self-serving personal agenda?
- Is One part of a group that is more concerned with doing things to be seen than being present at the moment and acting without expectation?
- Is One fearful that if One doesn't say 'yes' or participate that One will not be part of a particular relationship, friendship circle or social group?

If One answered 'yes' to any of these questions, it is highly likely that One's life is driven by One's ego and not aligned with One's inner spirit, soul or cosmic consciousness. The other sure way to test if a situation is likely to attract oneself down an egoic path is the simple 'feel good' awareness check.

Depending on the situation, circumstance or event, check in with One's mind–body about a question or path that One is about to take in life. Pause for a moment and ask oneself 'Is this decision right for One?' Then observe One's mind–body intuitive response or 'gut feeling'. If it 'feels right', then it will 'feel right' within One's stomach! Go ahead with the action. Act with confidence and enjoy whatever comes next. If it doesn't 'feel right', review, reflect and reassess and maybe wait, or choose an alternative path at the time.

Another important life tool is to acquire and engage with a good mentor, life coach or spiritual guide to help One along 'the way'. Seek out people who have 'been there and done that'. One can learn from these people what not to do and what is the best path to take. A good mentor will always make time to share One's insights and wisdom with others who are genuinely interested in learning to be a better version of oneself in life. Great mentors willingly share tricks, hints and tips about how to navigate obstacles, create solutions and be mindfully balanced in finding the right direction to reach the best outcome in life.

People who live a quality awakened life are often imbued with spiritual values and inner virtues. These individuals will act with a higher level of spiritual authenticity and integrity than others. This is in part because these humans have realised that all life is an illusion and know the difference between the imaginary false truths of ego and the 'real reality' of life in the world. People of this nature seek not to sell something to others but to share One's gifts with the world.

Journeying along One's way in life will require One to figure out how to navigate the space within One's mind and body as well as the interdimensional reality of One's spirit, soul or cosmic consciousness. In doing this, One will also need to navigate the world that One lives in today. Not everything will come with instructions; in fact, most situations, activities, events and personal relationships will not have a manual or easy assembly guide. One will need to draw upon the learnings, teachings and pointings of great masters, elders, important thinkers, thought-leaders and change-makers as well as family, friends, partners, kin, community and First Nation. No single person will have all the answers or solutions that One is likely to need on One's life journey on Earth.

This is why it will be critically important to trust One's spirit. Hopefully, this book will give One the courage, motivation and inspiration to help One work through anything that is not working out for oneself now.

Simply make time to:
1. Pause – stop hurting, harming, hindering or being unhelpful to oneself.
2. Review – sense and observe if One is being driven by an egoic agenda or internal egoic mental programming.
3. Reorganise – start to create a new space to realign One's life so that it is spirit-centric.
4. Repurpose – seek to meditate and intentionally act mindfully to be in a coherent mind–body–spirit state of existence throughout One's life.
5. Recommit – sync One's daily life and actions so that they align with One's spirit and 'the way' of the universe.

Seeking the right way to self-realisation, inner awakening and divine enlightenment

Self-realisation, inner awakening and divine enlightenment are important because they represent the process of understanding and uncovering One's true spiritual nature, purpose, and potential in life. When an individual is on this path, One can experience a profound sense of fulfillment, joy and inner peace. This journey can also have a positive impact on humanity as a whole, as each person who achieves a higher level of consciousness contributes to creating a more harmonious, compassionate, and loving world on Earth.

There are many benefits from seeking the right way to self-realisation, inner awakening and divine enlightenment.

Greater self-awareness

By embarking on this journey, individuals can gain a deeper understanding of oneself and One's emotions, beliefs, thoughts, attitudes, habits and behaviours. This self-awareness can help One identify areas where One needs to grow, change and improve, as well as recognise One's strengths, resilience, abilities, skills, gifts and talents.

Increased compassion and empathy

As individuals become more in tune with One's inner selves, One often develops greater empathy, kindness and compassion for others in life. This can lead to a more positive and supportive community, as people become more willing to help and support each other.

Improved relationships

By developing greater self-awareness and compassion, individuals can also improve One's friendships, partnerships, relationships and wellships with others. One may become a better listener, more patient and more understanding, which can lead to stronger, more fulfilling connections, meaningful relationships and an overall increase in quality of life.

Greater sense of purpose

Through self-realisation and inner awakening, individuals can discover One's true spiritual purpose in life. This can give One a sense of direction and motivation, as One works towards achieving One's goals and making a positive impact in the world today.

Inner peace and contentment

As individuals progress on One's spiritual journey, One will often experience a sense of inner peace and living contentment in life. This can lead to greater happiness and fulfillment, as One finds joy in the present moment and is less attached to material possessions or external circumstances.

Profound benefits are possible for both the individual and humanity as a whole when One is being guided by One's spirit and flowing with 'the way' of the universe. A more positive and harmonious world can be manifested when the people of this planet align in spiritual unity with a common purpose to free oneself and create a better and brighter future.

However, the only path of freedom to self-realisation and inner awakening is the one that One consciously chooses now. When One makes the choice to free oneself of One's ego and step into the light of self-realisation, this is the moment that an interdimensional doorway will open to a new way of seeing, perceiving and experiencing the world that One currently lives in today.

No other person can choose to awaken somebody else so that they may be free. One must intentionally choose this path and way of being for oneself. As soon as One makes the choice to free oneself, the path will appear before One now.

Know that no temples, churches, sacred rituals, divine spaces or even holy texts are required to enable One's way and spiritual path in life. It is not even necessary to have a spiritual guru or enlightened teacher. There is no special requirement for enlightenment or for truth-seekers to commit to a vision quest or undertake great acts of suffering in order to prove oneself worthy of receiving any special divine knowledge or gaining entry to the secrets of the universe.

However, there are definite benefits in seeking out the words and wisdom of truly awakened people both in the past and present on the planet now. Never underestimate the universe's innate and inherent ability to guide along the path to inner realisation and awakening. One simply needs to remain open, receptive, spiritually centred and genuinely present in the moment.

Being part of a religious or cultural group does have collective benefits. However, it can often shield oneself from knowing the truth of One's own spiritual existence in this life. Practicing a particular religion is often about accepting and relying on the truth of someone else's spiritual experience. It is not about finding, accepting and experiencing One's own spiritual truth in the world. Over the years, various religions have been perverted by the state and church. Both have used religion to fuel egoic agendas of segregation, isolation, hate, control and power. This has led to great religious wars, the conquest of new worlds and horrific acts of genocide and enslavement of First Nations' people in the name of 'God', 'Allah' or the 'Almighty'.

The same religious doctrine, belief and faith does not live in everyone on the planet. However, individual spirituality is the same and exists in every sentient Being on Earth. This is the major difference.

The intellectual and social comfort that One feels when One follows others or blindly believes in a particular faith cannot compare to the overwhelming ecstasy and contentment that One experiences when One finally aligns in coherence with One's own spirituality. Seeking the right way is not like finding a book in a library or bookstore. It must be done within the context of One's current life or contemporary lifestyle.

Just as rainbows appear in the sky when the conditions are right, so too will 'the way' when One has created a space for and daily commitment to this new way of living life. Some people believe that change is hard – and so it will be. However, others believe that change or changing is effortless when One lets go and goes with the flow of life – and so this will be too. Both perceptions are correct for the people observing oneself and imagining One's perceived or potential outcome.

Life is change and the changes that One will experience in this lifetime all lead people back to Source. Learning to choose the right path in the moment requires ongoing external assessment and inner alignment. It takes time to know, practice to get right and a commitment to One's spirit, soul or cosmic consciousness.

> **To the universe, all reality is virtual. It has no planned agenda, only to know itself.**

This is why everything can be created out of nothing and nothing exists within everything that is created. All things that appear real are nothing more than perceived illusions in space and time. Eventually all matter and energy or altered consciousness will be folded into itself and be repurposed in the universe. The universe uses all that is, and all that is, is an integral part of the universe.

Like a mighty river flowing out to sea, the universe has a divine current and this is 'the way' for all things in it. One is unable to escape, only flow with it along 'the way'. The more One resists it, tries to fight it or struggles against it, the more One will lose One's way in life. However, the more One feels it, flows with it and recognises that One is part of this beautiful experience, the more One's life will be in balance and harmony with all living things.

Effortlessness is not about getting everything right to make One's life easy. It is recognising that life is already 'easy' when One adopts a mindful attitude of gratefulness, abundance and effortlessness with 'the way' of the universe.

Notice how the waves crash effortlessly on a beach, or how a river flows effortlessly out to sea, or how a mountain stands in quiet silence. Look at these things and realise that nature does everything without effort and yet all things exist in synergy with everything on Earth. First Nations' people have known this for millenniums. It is time to relearn this wisdom now too.

Every time One finds oneself stressed or notices One's frustration levels rising, take a moment to consciously pause, stop whatever One is doing and take a breath. Do not do anything. Create space in One's life, learn how to just sit quietly, close One's eyes and calmly breathe. Focus only on One's breath, in and out, slowly, peacefully and calmly. Sense the rising and falling of One's chest as the air comes in and goes out. With every breath that One takes in – just … let … go … now.

This breathwork practice is a good starting point for managing One's life, participating in meditation sessions and aligning with One's spirit, soul or cosmic consciousness. One can undertake this breathwork anywhere on the planet when it is safe to do so. It is how great masters recentre oneself in times of activity, change or just completing daily tasks in One's life. The more One is able to integrate this kind of breath work meditation sessions into One's contemporary lifestyle or modern work-life activities, the greater One will be able to flow with 'the way' of the universe.

It will help One to shift One's life energy or 'chi' into a peaceful balanced state. It will also enable One to bring a sense of serene calm, quiet tranquillity and soothing gentleness into One's mind–body.

As One stops searching or seeking 'the right way', it will be present now. Knowing this is key to understanding that all One needs is the 'right intention' and all will be revealed to oneself. This is because One is not forcing a solution – it is already present within oneself. All One must do is 'get out of the way' by removing the veil of ego from within One's mind.

Great teachers and spiritual masters will not 'tell' or 'instruct' students exactly what to do in life. One can only lead or point 'the way' for others to discover the path within oneself. Ultimately, there is no greater teacher than the master that lives within every sentient Being on the planet.

> **Everyone must discover the divine light that shines within and bring this radiance to the world that One lives in today.**

Know that One has a great cosmic responsibility to oneself, others, the world, this planet, solar system, galaxy, other interstellar Beings and universe to shine as brightly as One can now.

Rising above it all to truly succeed as a spiritual Being of love, light and oneness

Rising above egoic stressors in this life is important for spiritual growth and success as it allows individuals to tap into One's true essence as spiritual Beings of love, light, and oneness. The ego is the part of the human psyche that is focused on the self and often creates stressors such as fear, anxiety, and attachment to material possessions. By letting go of these egoic stressors, individuals can connect to One's higher self, which will enable One to access and express love, compassion, kindness and wisdom. There are many benefits from rising above egoic stressors in daily life.

Increased inner peace

When individuals let go of the stressors created by the ego, they can experience greater inner peace, tranquillity and calmness. This allows One to be more present in the moment and fully enjoy these experiences.

Improved relationships

By rising above egoic stressors, individuals can develop a greater sense of empathy, kindness and compassion towards others in One's life and in the community. This can lead to improved personal and professional relationships, as One becomes more patient, understanding, mindful and loving towards others.

Increased creativity

When individuals let go of egoic stressors, One can tap into One's true creative potential. This allows One to express oneself more fully, completely and authentically, as well as explore new ideas and inspirational possibilities.

Greater sense of purpose

By connecting with One's higher self, individuals can discover One's true spiritual purpose and meaning in life. This can give One a greater sense of direction and motivation, as One works towards achieving One's goals and making a positive impact in the world.

> **Improved health**
>
> Letting go of egoic stressors can have mental and physical health benefits, such as reducing stress-related illnesses, promoting overall wellness and improving One's wellbeing and quality of life.

Realise the amazing and awesome impact of doing this in One's daily life. It increases inner peace, improves relationships, increases creativity, enables a greater sense of purpose and improves health and overall wellness in life.

To truly succeed in life is not about beating others at a competitive game or work task but in being the best version of oneself here and now. Success needs to be globally redefined in terms of living mindfully, loving openly, cooperating effectively, enabling creativity, sharing willingly, positively encouraging and being compassionate in the moment. The spiritual realm does not care how many material possessions or how much money in the bank One has. Neither money nor physical matter have any specific currency within consciousness itself. Frankly, it has no real, perceived or potential value at all. Spirit has no need of money or matter in any other dimension that it exists in now.

The only real currency in the spiritual realm is One's spiritual essence or divine synergy as a Being of light, love and oneness. Everything else is irrelevant.

When people leave Earth and re-enter the spiritual realm, they leave everything behind. As spirit, soul or cosmic consciousness, One will continue One's journey in the universe.

Many humans living in Western countries have been taught, trained and brainwashed into thinking that One must accumulate vast amounts of money, become wealthy or famous, aspire to be rich, work hard, get the best deal that One can, buy the biggest house, sacrifice One's health, wellbeing and wellships, suffer in silence, not share One's resources or energy, be individually focused, economically enslave other people and put oneself before others in the family or community in order to be happy and successful in life. Past messaging has been principally around working harder – not smarter, taking more – giving less, living faster – dying older, extracting and consuming individual experiences – not celebrating and creating shared ways of living life, promoting illness – devaluing wellness. Contemporary messaging with the newest generation on the planet – the millennials – is about entitlement, accelerated advancement and experiential necessities. These social constructs and living ideologies are part of an egoic false truth or ego-centric doctrine that has received prominence and popularity in the last two hundred years.

The internet and smartphones, and the recent global pandemic, have led to an increased use of social media, more online shopping and the propagation of an intensified consumer culture around the world.

There is a false notion circulating within the minds of people who seek to have it all. People with this mindless outlook and unconscious living operating system have very little regard for the environment and the overall adverse impact One's actions are having on Earth. These people are willingly ignorant of the issues of those in the community or society who are less fortunate. These individuals have no sense of spirit, soul or cosmic consciousness because One is operating from egoic programming seeking only to serve oneself in the fear of missing out.

This collective of individuals think, act and operate within a fear-based assumption or panicked survival mode. There is an underlying believe that One is constantly in a state of survival and if One does not act now, One is going to miss out or die tomorrow. Living life like this only fuels more fear, increases disharmony, promotes distrust, gives rise to illicit drug use and misuse, disrupts personal relationships, reduces quality rational conversations, raises mental health issues, diminishes cooperation and creativity, adds to child safety issues, concerns or worries, heightens social isolation and amplifies the occasions of domestic violence in society. It is a negative, low-vibrational energy cycle that feeds back upon itself to produce more of the same in the world.

The answer is simple. It requires One to look within oneself and come to terms with One's spirit, soul or cosmic consciousness. This is what the universe has been suggesting, encouraging, nudging and leading One to rediscover about oneself. It is 'the way' forward to a new future that is free from fear, pain and suffering in One's life.

It all begins with mindful self-awareness now. Creating space and time to get to know the real 'you' or sentient Being within One's human form. One needs to realise that One is **not** human – yes, that is right. Let's say it again: 'One is not a human being'. Just so we are clear here. What if this idea or concept is expressed in another way? One is a sentient Being of love, light and oneness hosting a human form (male, female, transgender or non-binary).

One has never been human, not since the time of One's birth on this planet. Some may say that this idea or perspective is pedantic or intellectually obscure – it is not.

The way in which One perceives oneself in life has an enormous effect on who One believes oneself to be now. It is the foundation upon which beliefs are built or created. It goes to the essence of who One is in the universe. It answers One of the most fundamental questions that most people living on Earth have about oneself : 'Who am "I"?' Or, better said this way: 'Who is One?'

> *You become what you believe, not what you think or what you want.*
> Oprah Winfrey

As One meditates on this spiritual realisation, a number of things will occur to oneself. If One's human form and thoughts are only part of an avatar to experience life on Earth, then One can change almost everything about this incarnated physical and mental construct. This is correct. One's human avatar or mind–body form can be changed within the quantum unified field or altered consciousness in which it currently exists. One can influence, shift, shape, configure and change the expressed energy signature of this human avatar into whatever One chooses. Amazing! Think about this idea for a moment.

With every thought that One thinks, One can influence the natural unified field of existence that is currently manifested as One's human form. This means that One can think oneself well, cure illness, create an aura of positivity and wellness around oneself, radiate a high electromagnetic field from One's heart out into the world, feel great, learn new things, create additional neural pathways in the brain as well as rewire it and extend One's life expectancy on Earth. The list goes on ... Anything is possible if One simply takes the time to explore and express oneself from this new perspective or point of view.

There is growing scientific evidence that supports these ideas and more. Having an open mind is the first step in letting go of old concepts or theories or attachments to outdated ways of thinking about oneself in this world. Quantum physics teaches that the 'observer effect' means that the act of observing influences the thing being observed and that the observation causes waves to turn into particles. The observer effect was validated with the double-slit experiment, which revealed that particles are in a state of potential until they are observed.

What this means for One's human avatar is that when One begins to observe it, the act of observation affects what is being observed. In other words, if One chooses to see One's human avatar through a lens of positivity, goodwill, wellness, love, light energy with a spirit, soul or cosmic consciousness at its core, this is exactly what One will observe in real life and real-time.

As One begins to practice and embed this perspective into One's daily life and outlook, amazing things will start to happen. One will find oneself having more energy, greater focus, increased stamina, being in a state of ongoing contentment and peace, shielded from the negative actions of others, drawn to the energy of positive radiant high-level vibrational people, and acting with a heightened sense of spiritual awareness and compassion.

One will also notice that One can now influence space and time differently. One may feel that One is able to predict or purposely plan the future. Ideas, activities and events seem to happen easily, with little effort, investment or energy. One could even experience multiple synchronicities happening in One's life again and again.

This changed outlook will give rise to changing the way that One experiences life on Earth. Some people may think that this is linked to a mystical or 'godly' process, but it is not. It is simply about accepting responsibility for One's life, spirit, thoughts, beliefs, behaviours, habits and actions plus One's mind–body. Some may reference the 'Law of Creation', 'Law of Intention', Law of Assumption' or the 'Law of Attraction'. But it is simply mastering the expression of the energetic quantum field or coherent mind–body–spirit of One's existence at this moment in space–time.

Knowing how One can affect One's own existence is key to reshaping, reconfiguring and redefining success in One's life. The journey of success is the destination that one should be focusing on. Success in every moment, throughout every aspect of One's life and in the way that One lives life in this world today. Success is not something that One puts off for another day. One creates it in everything that One does, thinks and says now.

Knowing when One has finally arrived

One's new and evolving future is being created at this moment now. As One works on oneself, with the help of other sentient Beings and visiting interstellar entities, One is manifesting a new and changed reality on Earth today. Nothing can stop the process of spiritual evolution on the planet. It is coming whether people like it or not. Being ignorant of this global paradigm shift in people's consciousness will not change the fact that an event horizon is fast approaching all citizens.

One hundred years from now, it is most likely this world will have a very different feel and look from what it has today. As people begin to wake up and realise the spiritual intelligence within oneself, from going through the 'global awakening process' people will naturally reorganise systems of shared beliefs, social–financial processes and human living-learning-earning practices to better align with an increased level of collective consciousness.

Some people are more advanced along the awakening process than others. But everyone everywhere will be exposed to it. This will change the planet and how people see oneself, others and interstellar visitors.

> *The religion of the future will be a cosmic religion. It should transcend personal God and avoid dogma and theology. Covering both the natural and the spiritual. It should be based on a religious sense arising from the experience of all things natural and spiritual as a meaningful unity.*
> Albert Einstein

The important question is not if this change is going to happen, but when. The ripple of spiritual evolution has already begun on the planet. It is now turning into a global spiritual tsunami that will be felt by all citizens of Earth. Every corner of the planet will be touched in some way by this dramatic paradigm shift in the collective consciousness of humanity.

A lot of people will try and run away or hide from it, but it will reach these individuals in the end. The change will be felt more on the inside than a visible effect on the outside of all people, across every country, every nationality or First Nation and will affect every man, woman and child on Earth.

One may ask: What is the outcome of this planetary change process for humanity? The answer is: The outcome of a spiritual evolutionary process on Earth will be the creation of a new manifested reality on the planet. This new future reality will be an interstellar spiritually based Type 1 civilisation on Earth.

Like any change in human society, there will be people that lead the process and there will be others that lag behind it. Governance structures are yet to be established that will be able to successfully navigate the transition to a new global culture, new world economy and new planetary social network. The people in charge today will have to reskill in order to manage the collapse of some existing systems and social structures. It will require thought-leaders and change-makers to come together in a spirit of cooperation and mutual benefit to support the change process.

Humanity stands on the precipice of interstellar spiritual evolutionary change. It will either destroy itself, resulting in the collapse of multiple ecosystems on Earth, or it will spiritually evolve and venture out amongst the stars. Whatever the outcome, it will require a conscious intentional decision, focused attention and applied effort to manifest either reality.

The good news is that humanity has the power, wisdom, insight, spiritual intelligence and awakened presence to save itself now. Within each individual sentient Being on Earth lies the seeds to be the best version of oneself and act as a spiritual ambassador and planetary custodian for all future generations.

The Earth cannot be owned by any single individual or nation-state – it belongs to all.

One has a moral, ethical and spiritual responsibility to protect the Earth for every generation, both now and in the future. This is the primary principal or living tenet of all First Nations' people: care for Country (land, sea and sky) as it gives life to One too.

As governments and international corporations continue to hide the truth of this spiritual evolution and reality from the citizens of Earth it will only create more confusion, chaos and conflict across the planet. People, corporations and governments with egoic values and agendas seek to muddy the waters of rational, well-balanced discussions and mature holistic conversations between ordinary people. They operate and instigate actions, laws and policies based on fear. In addition, this group of 'egosites' will actively and covertly try to manipulate the population into believing that moving to a totally new way of living, working, playing and being in this world is impossible. This is a blatant lie and a total fabrication made up of false facts and untruths. In the coming years and decades, there will be an increase in fake news designed to mislead people into thinking that One needs to surrender One's personal will, rights and fate into these people's hands without any questions.

Those individuals who are aware of these subversive tactics and awake to these methods of egoic manipulation will be able to consciously challenge and intentionally resist any and all fake and false information.

> **Awake and consciously mindful people will always be able to see the truth. The truth does not need to hide. The truth has no agenda. The truth is like the light of day, it shines so that One may find One's way in the world.**

As the growing tide of awake people continues to rise on the planet, it will reach a tipping point of 1 per cent that will trigger a global change in the overall perception of the rest of the people on Earth. This is what egoic extremists and egosites fear the most: the loss of One's power and control to manipulate the systems and governance structures in the world.

> **The power of humanity to spiritually evolve, change and raise the level of consciousness on the planet has been and will always be indomitable.**

It is an unstoppable force that is heading in only one direction: to become an interstellar spiritually united Type 1 civilisation on Earth.

The benefits of this change will be significant and incredibly profound. It will shift the perception of people at both a micro and macro level. As the process of change is implemented, a lot of people will experience some form of personal, social, cultural and economic levels of discomfort and disruption to One's everyday life. Do not fear this. It is a normal part of the process of planetary change and spiritual evolution.

The world as One currently knows it is yet to experience such an extinction-level event of its current reality. It is going to be dramatic and life-changing for the majority of people. The impact will last for a very long time, most likely into the next millennium and beyond.

Older generations, who have enjoyed the stability of the existing social order, financial systems and governance structures, will struggle significantly to understand this paradigm shift. This is for a range of reasons. The first is that approximately 80 per cent of people's brains are currently hard-wired into living an egoic lifestyle, so One's life is built upon this belief. The second is that most people will want to continue to live in denial and become angry at the loss of One's pre-existing life and living assumptions. One will not realise or fully embrace the idea that One needs to adapt and accept this new living reality. These people will assume that One does not have the capacity to change and rewire the neural pathways in One's own brain. This is because One believes One is powerless to change One's old ways, thoughts, habits and beliefs. One has subscribed to the idea and thought patterns of helplessness in One's life. But this is a false perception of oneself. It is not true now, and never has been.

However, there are a lot of people who are 'change ready' and actively seek to dismantle the old ways of doing business and living within an egoic construct.

> *The world as we have created it is a process of our thinking. It cannot be changed without changing our thinking.*
> Albert Einstein

The people of this world are thirsty for something to change in One's life. A change that enables a new reality and future on Earth today. In general, people are now ready in the world to embrace an interstellar spiritually united Type 1 civilisation on Earth.

Existing boards of major international corporations, above-top-secret intergovernmental global alliances, together with elite 'egosites' or people with egoic parasitic behaviour, are resisting this new future reality on the planet. This nefarious group of individuals have diverse and vested interests in operating in the shadows beyond the purview of normal democratic checks and balances. This is done to disguise both One's 'unfriendly' intentions and a worldwide global agenda of complete and total dominance to keep the human population on the planet ignorant and disempowered. The ultimate aim is to maintain ongoing systems of control, management and power. But this timeline is quickly coming to an end as more and more people awaken within to assert One's own spiritual sovereignty.

This crime against humanity has been willingly orchestrated over hundreds of years yet no person, corporation or government has been held accountable. The common goal for this syndicate of global criminals is to keep people in the dark about a lot of things, including:

- quantum energy generators, zero-point energy technologies, perpetual motion machines and perpetual energy generators
- gravity wave generating systems for interstellar travel using 'gravity attraction' and 'gravity wave displacement' devices
- anti-matter fusion reactors
- interstellar trans-dimensional vehicles and/or probes
- exotic 3D materials that are manufactured in zero gravity or space and programmable matter generators
- nanotechnologies for bioengineering and space exploration
- interdimensional transporter systems
- AI (artificial intelligence), plus artificial general intelligence (AGI) and synthetic androids/drones
- quantum field healing medical technologies
- consciousness enabling connectivity systems that can reach across this galaxy.

This is only a small fraction of the things that will be disclosed in the years and decades that are coming.

Any sufficiently advanced technology is indistinguishable from magic.
Arthur C. Clarke

As more and more people awake, One will become automatically aligned with One's spirit, soul or cosmic consciousness. This will also enable One to operate at a higher level of synchronicity in the universe. As One practices living, working and being in coherence with One's mind–body–spirit, One will be able to dramatically shift One's life in any direction that One chooses. The truth of every situation will be instantly revealed to oneself when One is fully present in the moment. The future will not appear as something that One needs to work hard for, it will simply appear as a potential stream of reality to be manifested in the present.

The following is an AI-generated response to being asked to list potential future interstellar technologies that would benefit humanity:

1. Faster-than-light travel: Enabling humans to travel to other star systems within a reasonable amount of time
2. Advanced propulsion systems: Improving spacecraft propulsion to allow for more efficient and effective travel through space
3. Habitat and life support systems: Providing sustainable living environments for humans in space
4. Advanced communication systems: Allowing for real-time communication across vast distances in space
5. Renewable energy technologies: Providing reliable sources of power in space
6. Asteroid mining and resource utilisation: Utilising resources in space to support human exploration and settlements
7. Artificial intelligence and robotics: Improving the ability to gather and analyse data, as well as performing tasks that are too dangerous or impractical for humans
8. Enhanced radiation protection: Protecting astronauts from harmful radiation exposure in deep space
9. 3D printing and advanced manufacturing: Providing the ability to produce and repair equipment in space
10. Medical technologies: Improving health and wellness for astronauts on long-duration missions

There is no rational reason for anyone to panic at this moment. It should come as no surprise that substantial and credible evidence of advanced alien or interstellar technology and extra-terrestrial artifacts currently exists on Earth now. Although access to these interstellar artifacts, technology and inter-planetary agreements is highly guarded and protected, they nevertheless exist in plain sight.

To some, these ideas and assertions may appear to belong in the realm of conspiracy theory or science fiction, but the validated real-life testimonials and personal accounts have now reached a level that is too overwhelming to be ignored.

Many may be forgiven for thinking that One is talking a completely foreign language or acting insanely against current mainstream thinking. To some extent, this will be true from a certain perspective. However, on the other hand, it will be perfectly natural for One to align with One's spirit, soul or cosmic consciousness in this way. One's daily awareness of life and living will be heightened and increased to a higher level of sensitivity and operating vibrational energy.

The further that One journeys along this path, the greater this new reality on Earth will be revealed and manifested as part of One's new way of life and spiritual lifestyle.

An interstellar spiritually united Type 1 civilisation on Earth is already being co-created today on the planet. This manifestation process will only increase at an exponential rate as new generations are awakened at an earlier age. People will see the truth in the spiritual evolution of all humanity – not just as a whimsical option, but as a conscious necessity to take One's rightful place amongst the stars.

There is no greater gift that One can give oneself than the gift to awaken completely.

And once you are awake, you shall remain awake eternally.
Fredrich Nietzsche

It is time One becomes fully present as a 'Bright' in this world. One's new future reality on Earth begins today – so be it now.

IMPORTANT LEARNINGS, TEACHINGS AND POINTINGS

Key ways to live life as spirit, soul or cosmic consciousness

01 With great power comes great responsibility; with simple action comes significant change. Learn to change One thought at a time, then turn this thought into action and keep moving forward in this way. A thought is just a thought and can be changed at any time or any place on the planet.

02 Trusting oneself, One's spirit and the universe requires One to take a leap of faith. When One finally does this, a great gateway of opportunity will be opened for oneself to explore and experience new things in this life, world and universe. It is not about having all the pieces to the puzzle of life already figured out. It is learning to believe that everything will work out for One in the end, no matter what happens.

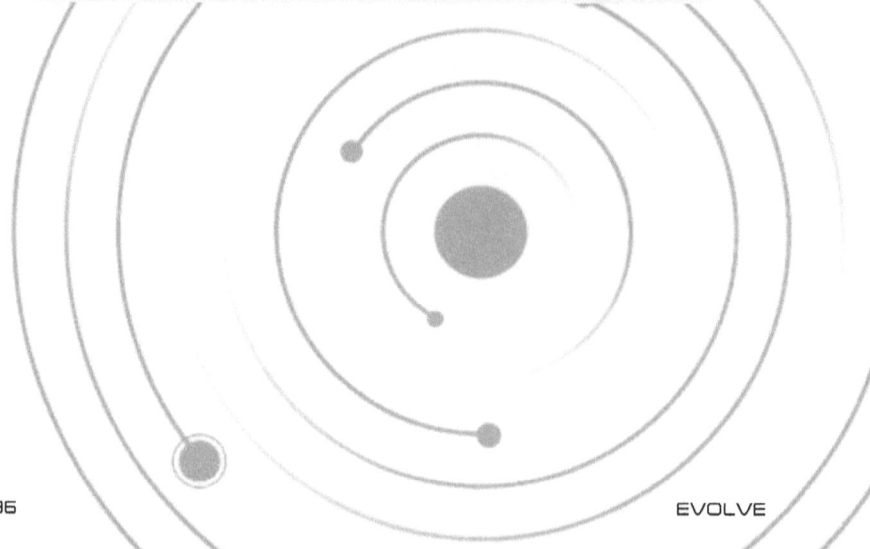

Simply make time to:
- pause – stop hurting, harming, hindering or being unhelpful to oneself
- review – sense and observe if One is being driven by an egoic agenda or internal programming
- reorganise – start to create a new space to realign One's life so that it is spirit-centric
- repurpose – seek to meditate and intentionally act mindfully to be in a coherent mind–body–spirit state of existence in One's life
- recommit – synch One's daily life so that it aligns with One's spirit and 'the way' of the universe.

As One stops searching or seeking 'the right way', it will be present now. Knowing this is key to understanding that all One needs is the 'right intention' and all will be revealed to oneself. This is because One is not forcing a solution; the solution is already present within oneself.

When One begins to observe it, the act of observation affects what is being observed. In other words, if One chooses to see One's human avatar through a lens of positivity, goodwill, wellness, love, light and divine energy with a spirit, soul or cosmic consciousness at its core, this is exactly what One will observe in real life.

The world is in the process of co-creating an interstellar spiritually united Type 1 civilisation on Earth today. It is time to fully embrace the idea that One needs to adapt and accept this new living reality now.

PART SEVEN

Living Life on Earth Now

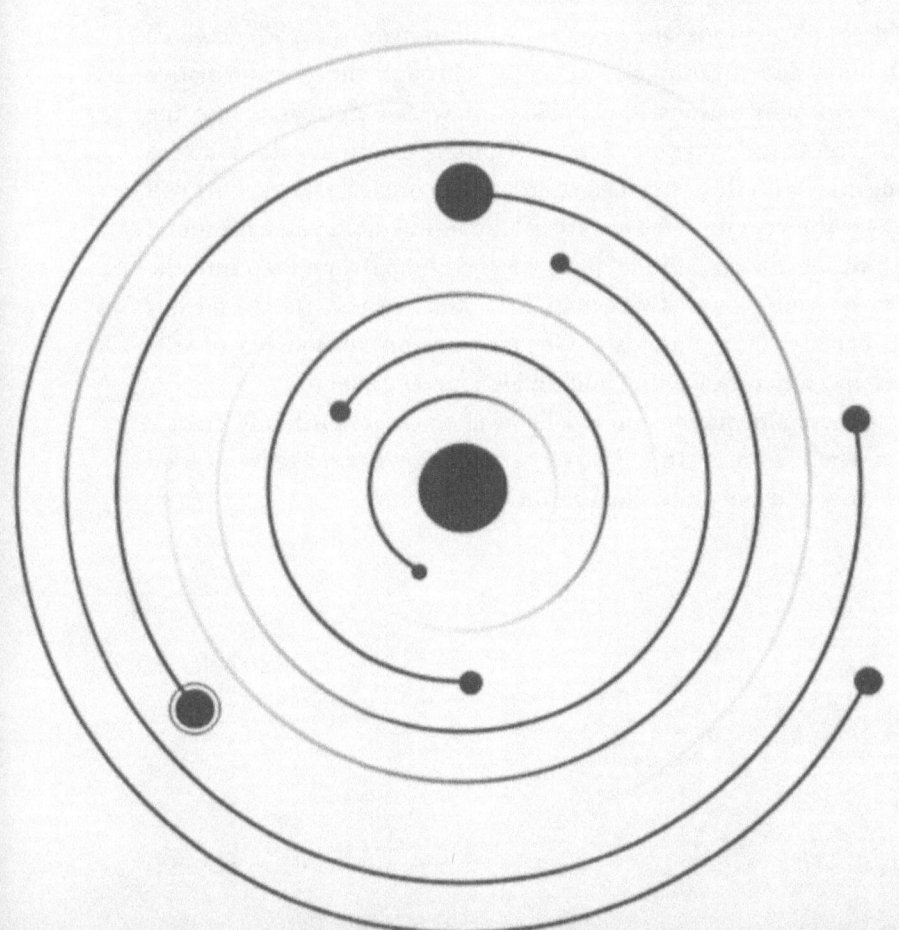

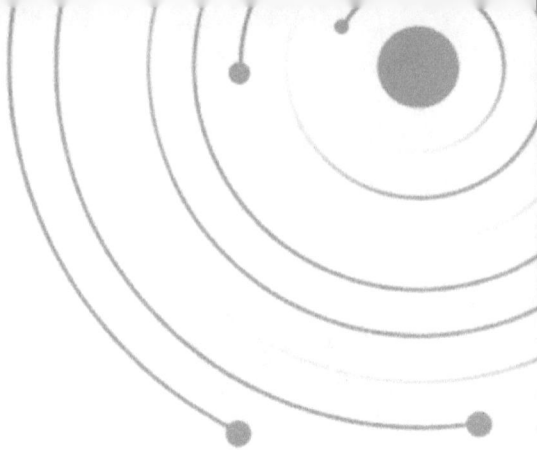

Affirmations for living a spiritual life now

In a world where distractions abound and challenges loom large, it is easy to forget the profound essence that resides within each and every person on Earth. However, hidden beneath the noise and chaos lies an extraordinary truth: within One, exists an infinite wellspring of potential waiting to be realised.

These affirmations are designed to illuminate the path towards a fulfilling and meaningful existence. Through the transformative practice of affirmations, this book empowers One to tap into the depths of One's spiritual Being, helping One to create a divine connection with the boundless energy of the universe. Here, One will discover the keys to living a spiritual life now, embracing a profound sense of self-love, gratitude, purpose and compassion. Step into the realm of One's own divine existence and witness the wondrous transformation that unfolds as One embarks on this journey of self-discovery, inner awakening and divine empowerment.

Use these affirmations on a daily basis to create profound change and a new life on Earth today. Write them down, say them out loud or silently and integrate them into One's life now.

Daily affirmations

One has got this because One confidently knows that One can do anything ...

One thanks the universe for the opportunity to be here and evolve

One loves and celebrates One's life and living presence on Earth

One is thankful for One's work, relationships and people that One shares this life experience with now

One is a vibration of coherent wellness (mind–body–spirit)

One is powerful beyond measure now and always

One is courageous, kind, caring and compassionate

One is able to achieve and become anything and everything in One's life

One is truly grateful for One's life on the planet

One is an amazing, wonderful, capable and resilient person

One is a sentient Being of light, love and oneness

One acts virtuously in what One thinks, says and does

One is a source of joy and love wherever One is in life

One is gentle, forgiving and understanding of oneself for not being perfect as a human being

One is safe, secure and worthy

One is at peace wherever One is in the world

One only focuses on the positive aspects of One's life each day

One attracts freedom, love, prosperity and abundance into One's life

One flows with ease and effortlessness in everything that One does

One expresses grace and humility

One honours and acknowledges the spirit, soul or cosmic consciousness in oneself and everyone

One works to manifest One's new vision, dreams and reality in the world today

One aligns in coherent synergy with mind–body–spirit and the universe

One is all of this and so much more now ...

PART EIGHT

Epilogue

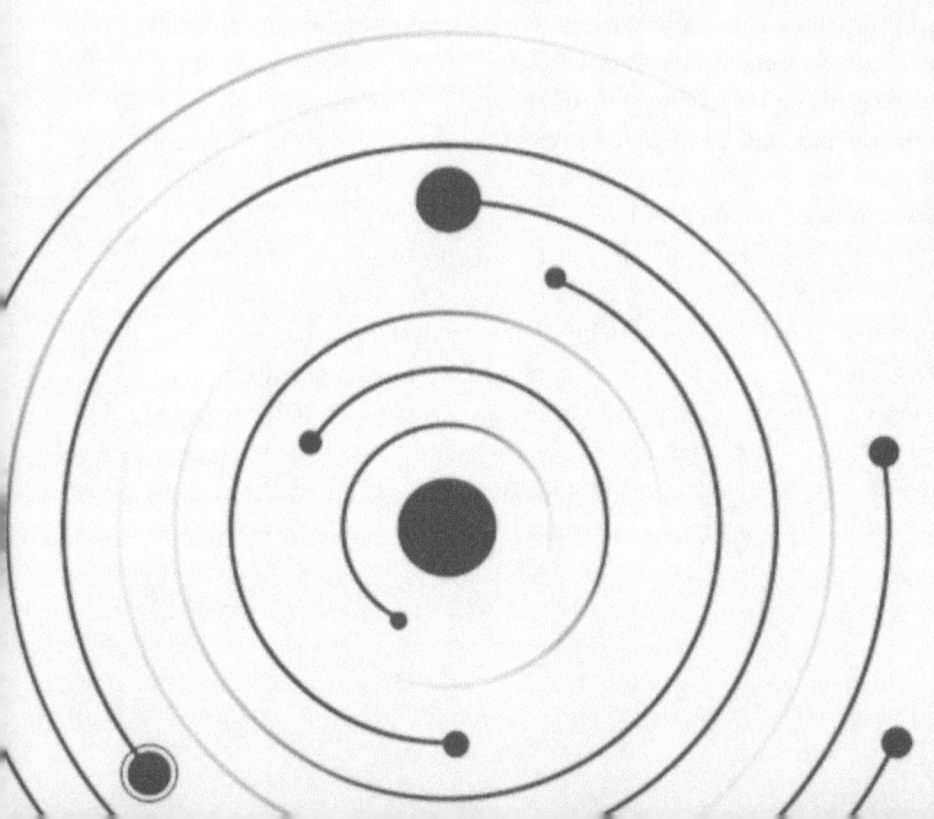

Manifesting the future

This future is now. Humans with egoic minds are all but extinct on the planet. Millions of people have woken up to a new interstellar spiritually based Type 1 civilisation on Earth. Life has consciously streamed forward towards the future, piercing the very fabric of space–time into the present. New generations of humans have come and gone like waves on the surface of the ocean. The mindless imprint of people's egoic beliefs, thoughts, behaviours, daily habits and lifestyles has been drowned out by the tide of spiritual truths and cosmic consciousness manifesting its awakening on Earth.

Eventually, a time came when the tipping point of human spiritual evolution was realised within all Beings. This changed everything and everything was changed by this moment. No One is exactly sure when the moment happened, nor can One pinpoint the exact day on which it occurred. But this does not matter now, as everyone is in a new manifested reality on Earth.

The 'language of One or spirit' and 'the way' of spirit, when learned from an early age, enables people to transcend time and eventually move beyond it. This is the catalyst, together with 'the great awakening', that created a planetary paradigm shift in the living consciousness of all human beings. People spiritually evolved and operated at a higher level of consciousness. This positive change altered everyone's relationship with oneself, each other, the world, interstellar Beings and the universe.

> **The Earth is at peace. There is no hunger or illness. There is no violence or war. The environment is healed and restored to its natural beauty. Honesty, kindness and compassion are practised by all.**

Free will and freedom are more than just words, they are a new way of working, living and being on Earth. The world evolved because people realised that One is spirit, soul or cosmic consciousness and chose to become awake at this moment.

Nobody can remember what it was like to be ego-centric, except for the 'Ancients' or 'Evolved Brights' that survived 'the great awakening' on the planet.

Like the sun moving across the landscape of humanity, the radiance of all life has been brightened due to the divine light within each sentient Being on Earth and interstellar visitors.

Incrementally, with each brand new day, people willingly upgrade One's human living operating system to align with One's higher self or enlightened spiritual consciousness. All over the world people have become intuitively aware of One's inner Being and the divine truth of the universe. The more people connect from a place of genuine goodwill and a sense of authentic spiritual intention, the more this raises the living consciousness and harmonic vibration of the entire planet. Like an endless ripple of invisible change, it spreads out in every direction, covering the Earth.

When One allows oneself to truly and deeply be present in the moment now, One may have strange or unusual feelings. As if everything is connected. Because it always was on Earth and in this galaxy. One may sense that One can see the whole spiritual evolution of humanity stretching out before One like a single long interconnected moment or series of interlinking events from the beginning. One might even feel as if One can see everything that has happened and is about to happen now.

Simply rest with this feeling of knowingness and allow oneself to be present with it. Let One's spirit, soul or cosmic consciousness guide One to a place and time where One is able to accept the vibration of this new reality and future being present now. Know that it is coming, realise that is already on its way. In fact, it is here now. There is nothing left to do other than accept it, embrace it, and live with it as part of One's evolved spiritual life.

Wherever One is, this is the place where it all begins. This is the moment when it all starts. It is time to change oneself and One's reality on Earth. A new interstellar future is manifesting now. Be the change that One seeks in life and so it will be.

Acknowledgments

Firstly, let me acknowledge all the people who enjoyed the books *One, Two, Three, Awaken* and *Infinite Existence*. It is with a deep sense of gratitude that One is thankful for all the positive feedback regarding how uplifting and inspiring these books have been in so many people's lives. Helping One's inner growth, personal change and spiritual transformation process to a better place of love, light and oneness is One of the best gifts One can enjoy in this world.

In bringing **Evolve** to life, One is genuinely appreciative of the many beautiful people One has met along the way. The journey of co-creating this new book has been a wonderful and inspiring experience.

If the contents of this book have resonated deeply within One's mind, body and spirit – so be it. This silent acknowledgement is the only confirmation that One needs to experience in order to realise a shift in alignment with One's higher spiritual self and true purpose in life.

It is with great humility and honour that One acknowledges the great spiritual teachers, thinkers, elders and masters who have committed to a life of sharing what One knows to be part of the essence of One's own inner truth. In doing so, One becomes a reflection of the divine Source, the Creator, the Supreme Being, God, Allah or the universe itself.

This book is a way of sharing One's teachings, learnings, pointings and powerful mindful practices that allow One to stop limiting thoughts, beliefs and behaviours, and start experiencing an aligned life that is manifested in the present moment and centred within One's spirit, soul or cosmic consciousness.

One is committed to One's inner peace and living contentment through the natural alignment and living coherence of mind, body and spirit with 'the way' of the universe.

To honour One's spirit is to acknowledge all spirits. To honour 'the way', is to acknowledge the divine flow of the universe. To honour now, is to acknowledge the beingness of One's eternal presence and infinite existence.

One is grateful for all the readers of this book, for whom this journey has been a transformative process along the path of spiritual inspiration, conscious awakening and universal alignment within.

May an inner way to peace, prosperity and contentment be realised and awakened within One now.

As One believes in One's spirit, soul or cosmic consciousness. One is evolving to co-create a new interstellar spiritually united Type 1 civilisation on Earth now. Being part of this future, begins the moment One believes in this reality today.

Other books by Shawn Wondunna-Foley

Associated study guides

www.ingramcontent.com/pod-product-compliance
Lightning Source LLC
Chambersburg PA
CBHW020318010526
44107CB00054B/1893